4

THE ENGLISH CRAFT GILDS AND THE GOVERNMENT

AN EXAMINATION OF THE ACCEPTED THEORY REGARDING THE DECAY OF THE CRAFT GILDS

STUDIES IN HISTORY, ECONOMICS AND PUBLIC LAW

EDITED BY THE FACULTY OF POLITICAL SCIENCE OF
COLUMBIA UNIVERSITY

Volume XXIII] [Number 4

THE ENGLISH CRAFT GILDS AND THE GOVERNMENT

AN EXAMINATION OF THE ACCEPTED THEORY REGARDING THE DECAY OF THE CRAFT GILDS

BY

STELLA KRAMER

AMS PRESS
NEW YORK

COLUMBIA UNIVERSITY
STUDIES IN THE
SOCIAL SCIENCES

61

The Series was formerly known as *Studies in History, Economics and Public Law.*

Reprinted with the permission of Columbia University Press
From the edition of 1905, New York
First AMS EDITION published 1968
Manufactured in the United States of America

Library of Congress Catalogue Card Number: 68-56666

AMS PRESS, INC.
New York, N.Y. 10003

PREFACE

THE conclusions presented in the following pages were reached as the result of an investigation of the relations commonly supposed to have existed between the English government and mediæval craft gilds, as shown especially in a series of statutes enacted in the fifteenth and sixteenth centuries, to which a great influence has hitherto been ascribed in the decay of English craft gilds.

The present study had its beginning at the University of Pennsylvania under the direction of Professor Edward P. Cheyney, who held that three factors should be taken into account in considering the decay of those organizations: First, internal divisions in craft gilds; secondly, external changes in the distribution of industry, shown by the rise of the "domestic system" of manufacture; and thirdly, the hostility or intrusion of the national government, indicated by a series of acts from 1436 to the Elizabethan Statute of Apprentices of 1563, by which the gilds were deprived of their administrative, legislative and jurisdictional freedom, as well as superseded in many of their economic functions.

Nor is Professor Cheyney alone in the stress thus laid upon legislative action. Various writers upon craft gilds have emphasized more or less the influence of such government intrusion. Professor Ashley sees as a factor in the weakening of industrial organization in the towns the increased action of the central authority, while Hibbert goes so far as to attribute an utter change in craft gilds as a whole, to one of these acts, that of 1563.

Such conceptions of the policy of the English government, however, show an apparent contradiction in its action relative to the gild system. On the one hand the state would seem to have favored the old towns by trying to check the growth of industry outside of their jurisdiction, by passing laws to regulate the processes of manufacture in different industries as they rose, and in some of these acts by giving power to gild officers to enforce state regulation. Yet in others, by the act of 1563 for example, craft authorities were entirely ignored, and thus the old trade organizations were supposedly superseded in the exercise of much of their work. Again, by the series of acts already referred to, freedom of action of the gilds was restricted by the requirement to submit their by-laws to the inspection and endorsement of government officials before they might be put into execution. It is these latter acts which have been held of especial importance in the decay of the gild system.

A detailed study of the relations which existed between the English government and craft organizations has failed to corroborate such views of the influence of any state action upon the gild system, and has led the writer to a view entirely opposed to that which she previously had held in keeping with the theories of Professor Cheyney and others. This has perhaps been but the natural result of a more extended study of the subject and a more complete isolation of the history of craft gilds. On the other hand the results have been made possible only by the thoroughness of training and the excellent methods of work derived from Professor Cheyney, to whom I have been much indebted throughout this investigation.

I wish also to express my thanks to Professor James

H. Robinson, of Columbia University, for much insight into historical perspective; to Professor Edwin R. A. Seligman and Professor Herbert L. Osgood for their encouragement and good counsel, and to Professor Merrick Whitcomb, of the University of Cincinnati, for similar assistance. In the final revision I have been greatly helped by Miss Louise R. Loomis, of Barnard College.

STELLA KRAMER.

NEW YORK, APRIL, 1905.

CONTENTS

INTRODUCTION

CHAPTER I

POLICY OF THE GOVERNMENT WITH REFERENCE TO CRAFT GILDS

CHAPTER II

POLICY OF THE EARLY TUDORS TOWARD CRAFT GILDS

CHAPTER III

LATER TUDOR POLICY AS A FACTOR IN THE DECAY OF CRAFT GILDS

CHAPTER IV

ENGLISH ECONOMIC POLICY IN THE MIDDLE AGES.

INTRODUCTION

DR. STUBBS has doubtless testified for all time to the value and great interest which the history of institutions has for those who, as he puts it, "have courage to work upon it."[1] Of no institution, perhaps, can this be more truly affirmed than of English craft gilds. In its broadest conception a study of those organizations involves the entire social history of England. In a stricter sense it narrows itself into a survey of the development of burghal interests and ambitions after the Norman Conquest, since it was in its boroughs that England's commercial and industrial life centered.

That the Norman duke realized to the very fullest degree the worth of his "conquest," Domesday Survey testifies; especially when it shows that, with the exception of the towns bestowed upon his favorite nobles or influential clergy, he had retained as his particular dominion the cities and boroughs of England.[2] But he lost no time in showing his willingness to propitiate the most royal of all his boroughs when he granted London a charter confirming her citizens in all the law whereof

[1] *Constitutional History*, vol. i, Preface.

[2] Jenks calls attention to the fact that the "conquest" places property much more at the disposal of its master than the heritage or office. *Law and Politics in the Middle Ages*, p. 39. Maitland classifies Domesday boroughs as royal and mediatized. *Domesday Book and Beyond*, pp. 212-218. See Ballard, *Domesday Boroughs*, pp. 9-10, for a list of Domesday boroughs.

they had been worthy in King Edward's day.[1] To the series of Anglo-Norman charters, through which from that time burgesses gradually obtained the privileges they desired and emancipated themselves from feudal control, we owe our knowledge of the growth of English towns.[2] During this process their political and commercial influence, keeping pace with the amount of corporate unity developed within their borders, gradually gained from the ruling powers the recognition that the boroughs were distinct forces in the land, and as such worthy of especial attention and privilege. What these privileges were, and how they became one by one chartered rights, by either royal or baronial favor, extant records amply testify.

One of the earliest of borough privileges thus recorded was the concession to burgesses in various towns of their gild merchant.[3] The significance of such an article in a twelfth century charter is not really apparent until we later see the institution in full operation. Then we appreciate the worth of the grant to the townsmen of the right to bind themselves in an association which

[1] For William's sole surviving charter, see Norton, *Commentaries*, p. 257.

[2] According to Miss Bateson, *Mediaeval England*, p. 271, the privileges chiefly sought were "liberty to manage their own finance, their own judicature, their own trade, freedom from the interference of the king's officers; and out of them the towns began to develop their councils, their courts, and powers of self-government of every kind."

[3] Henry II's charter to Oxford reads as follows: "Sciatis me concessisse et confirmasse civibus meis in Oxenforde omnes libertates et consuetudines et leges et quietantias quas habuerunt tempore regis Henrici avi mei, nominatim gildam suam mercatoriam cum omnibus libertatibus et consuetudinibus in terris et in silvis, pasturis, et aliis pertinentiis, ita quod aliquis qui non sit de gildhalla aliquam mercaturam non faciet in civitate vel suburbiis nisi sicut solebat tempore regis Henrici, avi mei . . ." Stubbs, *Select Charters*, p. 167.

exempted them from the payment of trade tolls and gave them the monopoly and regulation of all commercial interests within their domains. This was a royal privilege at that time, and as such, no doubt, right royally paid for. It is, moreover, most valuable testimony to the fact that English boroughs were profiting commercially and industrially by the incoming of the Normans. The desire or need for such an organization registers that fact for us,[1] and its authorization by royal charter lends to the mediæval gild merchant special significance as an English institution.

Association of men for the purpose of advancing common interests is a universal phenomenon of human society, indeed the very foundation of society itself. The fundamental principle underlying all such unions is invariably the same,—desire for co-operation—but the form in which that principle is expressed naturally varies with the conditions the association is established to meet and further. So in the industrial world there have doubtless always been unions of artisans, in all ages and among all peoples. In recognition of this fact we no longer attempt to trace the direct descent of English industrial gilds from earlier associations, such as the Roman colleges of workmen.[2] Given a body of men vitally concerned with the development of a particular interest, what will they do to promote it? History has and will unfailingly

[1] "Not until there was something of importance to protect," says Professor Gross, "not until trade and industry began to predominate over agriculture within the borough, would a protective union like the Gild Merchant come into being." *Gild Merchant*, vol. I, p. 4.

[2] Professor Seligman in his *Two Chapters on Mediaeval Gilds*, p. 50, considers this part of the subject, and establishes an absolutely independent origin for English gilds. Professor Ashley also discusses this phase in an interesting manner. *English Economic History*, vol. ii, pp. 77, 78.

record one answer. They will of their own accord draw together into an association rendered necessary and profitable by the state of society which called it into being.

It is, then, not this general principle leading to association but the particular form which the first attempt at industrial organization assumed in England with which we are concerned. This seems to have been the gild merchant. Just how great a rôle co-operation in trade had played in that country before the Norman conquest is not easy to determine. Some cities and boroughs had undoubtedly important commercial relations. London in the time of Athelstan had use for eight moneyers; Canterbury required six, and many other towns supported smaller numbers.[1] The merchant was protected; special inducements and emoluments were provided for his encouragement.[2] There were also distinct market regulations, traces of which may be found among Anglo-Saxon records,[3] although the idea of conceding to a community the right of association for the complete monopoly of trade seems not to have obtained before the creation of the gild merchant.[4] Nevertheless, the rapidity with which that institution spread through-

[1] Maitland, *op. cit.*, p. 195.

[2] A doom of that time ordains that a merchant who had made three long sea voyages on his own account should be entitled to the rank of a thane. This shows how great a national concern the encouragement of commerce had become. Norton, *op. cit.*, p. 21.

[3] Kemble, *Saxons in England*, vol. ii, p. 73, 328.

[4] Professor Gross has found no trace of a gild merchant in any of the Anglo-Saxon records, and therefore concludes that it was a new institution for England, probably introduced from Normandy. This is the view held by Norton also. The earliest distinct mention of it in extant English records is found in the charter granted the burgesses of Burford, in Oxfordshire, some time between 1087–1107. *Op. cit.*, vol. i, pp. 4, 5, 191.

out the land testifies to the development of England's commercial and industrial life.

Following closely upon the earliest known gild merchant there appeared another species of gild in certain of of the boroughs. During the later years of Henry I, Exchequer rolls testify to the payment by various artisan unions in London, Oxford and Lincoln for recognition of their right to have gilds.[1] That such a privilege during the twelfth century was exclusively a royal gift Henry II's Exchequer proves by its allusions to artisan gilds daring enough to establish themselves without such permission, which were detected and brought to terms.[2] By this time, moreover, legitimate gilds are evident in various other boroughs, especially in Nottingham, York and Winchester. Most of these were associations of weavers and fullers, results of the growth of the cloth industry; but a few other trades appear, more especially in London, where only (with the exception of the Oxford cordwainers) do such trades as the bakers, saddlers and goldsmiths appear important enough to have their unions recognized. Beyond the mere fact of their existence little is known of these earliest artisan gilds, except that they required royal permission to form at all. But in spite of their crown grant or, perhaps, because of it, their presence within some of the boroughs was evidently resented, and to such an extent that their members were refused the usual privileges of burgesses.

[1] A Pipe Roll of 31 Henry I, records payment by the weavers of Oxford, of two marks of gold that they might have their gild, while those of Lincoln were amerced for one mark only. Stubbs, *op. cit.*, vol. i, p. 412.

[2] These were the so-called adulterine gilds, so designated because "set up without Warrant." For so, according to Madox, "'tis explained in subsequent records referring expressly to this great Roll of the 26th year." *History of the Exchequer*, vol. i, p. 562.

This spirit of burghal hostility directed chiefly against gilds of weavers and fullers in such places as London, Oxford, Winchester, and in some of the less important towns as Beverley and Marlborough,[1] has in modern times been made the basis of the earliest theory of the origin of English craft gilds. Other views, wholly or partially opposed to the first, have since been put forward until we have now practically three methods of accounting for the rise of that institution. Brentano and his followers, the first in the field, arguing from the ill-feeling shown in the boroughs just referred to, and drawing upon analogies furnished by Continental conditions, ascribe the origin of English craft gilds to the expulsion from the greater gild, or gild merchant, of the artisans, who were thus led to form unions of their own.[2] Professor Gross and his adherents, on the contrary, contend that the hostility in some towns was wholly exceptional, that artisans, generally speaking, were freely admitted to the gild merchant in most English boroughs, and that the rise of craft gilds was a spontaneous movement of the fourteenth and fifteenth centuries.[3] The exceptional instances of exclusion Mr. Gross explains as due probably to jealousy against Flemish intruders. Regarded as

[1] The weavers and fullers of Oxford, for example, were "not to weave or full any cloth that is their own without the leave of the proved men of the town," upon pain of forfeit of the cloth. No freeman could be "attainted" by a weaver or fuller, nor could they "bear any witness." Besides such restrictions from Beverley records it seems that "if any one wishes to forswear his craft let him deal with him who is called mayor and with the bailiffs of the town, that he may be received into the franchise of the town; and let him remove the looms from his house. And this law they have in the franchise of London as they say." *Liber Custumarum*, p. 131. See, also, *Beverley Town Documents* (*Selden Society Publications*), p. 135, for a more correct version of these laws.

[2] Smith, *English Gilds*, cxv.

[3] *Gild Merchant*, vol. i, p. 117.

aliens, they were refused admission to civic and mercantile franchises.[1] Professor Ashley, however, takes a middle position, asserting that there is no reason to believe that these artisans were of Flemish blood, and excluded on that ground from borough privileges. He believes that the relation which existed between the gild merchant and the artisans within the English boroughs was by no means so harmonious as Professor Gross would have us suppose.[2]

However, all that we really know about the matter is that there was this opposition shown toward weavers and fullers in the towns already mentioned, and that it took the form of barring them, as long as they exercised their trades, from the usual rights of free burgesses. The

[1] *Ibid.*, p. 108. See Ochenkowski, *Englands wirthschaftliche Entwickelung im Ausgange des Mittelalters*, pp. 58-62. Cunningham, *Growth of English Industry and Commerce*, vol. i, pp. 176-182. *Liber Custumarum*, Introd. lxi, for the same view of their foreign origin.

[2] He refutes Professor Cunningham's view of their foreign origin, and discusses the question in his review in the *Political Science Quarterly*, vol. vi, p. 155. For Ashley's explanation of the rise of craft gilds, see *English Economic History*, vol. i, p. 80. Professor Seligman, in his *Two Chapters*, p. 58, also opposes the supposition of a foreign origin, and considers these as exceptional cases which from the outset were regarded with disfavor by the gild merchant. This latter statement, however, raises the question, worthy perhaps of some emphasis, which seems not to have attracted attention heretofore, namely, whether the opposition directed against these early artisans did not proceed rather from the burgesses as a whole, than from the organized gild merchant. What significance may lie in this, cannot be decided at this time, but burgess-ship and membership in the gild merchant were by no means identical terms in the earliest stages of a town's development. "The test of burgess-ship may well have been one thing in the year 1000, another in 1200, another in 1300. By 1400, to enter the gild merchant of Leicester . . . was to enter the freedom of the borough; but in 1300 a distinction between the gildsman and the burgess is still so far visible as to make it likely that in 1200 it was obvious." Bateson, *Records of Leicester*, vol. i, Introd. xxviii.

precise period when this spirit of hostility was displayed towards those handicraftsmen is by no means certain, since the date of the records has not been established beyond dispute.[1] Nor can the cause of this burghal ill will be easily determined in the absence of sufficient evidence to warrant our attributing it to a foreign nationality. In any event no single explanation can suffice for conditions so widely prevalent, nor can it account for the rise of craft gilds as an English institution. It may well be that the right even though derived from the crown to establish a gild in boroughs where the citizens as a whole already enjoyed in their gild merchant a monopoly and oversight of all trade, would be sufficient occasion for borough dissatisfaction. This partial duplication of powers would naturally bring the two associations at some point into conflict. It was an *imperium in imperio* in the community's industrial world, and consequently very likely to breed dissension.[2]

[1] We have evidence now which may help to determine this vexing question of the period when artisan gilds first evoked town antagonism. Heretofore investigators have depended wholly upon the account in *Liber Custumarum*, which contains warrant for the supposition that expressions of ill will belonged to the later thirteenth century. In formulating her hypothesis the writer had only that evidence to draw upon. She has discovered since, among the publications in the *London Municipal Collection of Documents*, from original manuscripts in the British Museum (*English Historical Review*, vol. xvii, p. 509), references to these early Norman-French gild laws which fix their date as no later than the ninth year of King John. Moreover in the volume of *Beverley Town Documents*, edited for the Selden Society, Mr. Leach has incorporated copies of these laws taken from the British Museum collection. In connection with them he remarks that the character of the handwriting in which the laws were written fixes their date somewhere in the last quarter of the twelfth century. (Introd., xlv.) If that be the epoch of borough antagonism, there is new ground for the argument that hostility to the artisan gilds came rather from the town than from the gild merchant.

[2] One cannot but wonder whether Henry II was not providing against

Nevertheless, whatever the correct explanation may be of the rise and status of these earliest known artisan gilds, their history can by no means be taken as typical in dealing with that system of craft gilds which arose later in the thirteenth and the following centuries, and which as it developed, dominated the English industrial world for centuries. It is the failure to appreciate this fact, perhaps, which is responsible for the confusion that exists in regard to the rise and development of the gild system as a whole, where one must take into consideration chiefly the gild merchant and the later craft gilds. What is the true view of their relationship? Herein lies the point of contention among writers upon the subject, and the obscurity in which it has been involved has led to the various conceptions of a hostile spirit supposedly existing between the two species of gild organization.

The publication within the last few years of the *Leicester Borough Records*, containing the earliest extant gild merchant rolls, enables us to see something of the real connection between the two classes of industrial organizations in that borough, at least, and affords a basis for

this contingency when in confirming Oxford's right to have a gild merchant he granted its members the sole privilege of exercising trade within the town and suburbs "nisi sicut solebat tempore regis Henrici avi mei" (except as was customary in the reign of Henry I, my grandfather). To whom did this exception refer if not to the gilds of weavers and cordwainers which had in the reign of Henry I obtained recognition by the customary method, namely, a payment into the king's treasury? Is this not proof that the Oxford gild merchant had no power to make trade regulations for those gilds or to exercise supervision over their immediate interests? After all, was not the manifestation of antagonism the protest of the borough rather than of the gild merchant against the existence of separate gilds? Since weavers and fullers seem in most of the towns to have been the only trades able to purchase gild privileges, their associations were made to bear the brunt of burghal disapproval.

conjecture as to the normal mode of gild development throughout the country.

Leicester, probably one of the most important midland boroughs, appears after the Conquest as the property of Robert, Count of Meulan, Henry I's chief confidant. Conveniently situated for commercial intercourse, with perhaps an added importance from its former standing as one of the five Danish burghs, Leicester early in the twelfth century obtained from its lord the grant of a gild merchant.[1] Just how soon the men of that borough took advantage of this privilege does not appear. The earliest gild roll preserved bears date of 1196; this indicates that by that time, at least, men of every trade then known enjoyed the privilege of enrolling themselves within its membership.[2] They paid the entrance fee, pledged obedience to gild rules and promised attendance at all its meetings. Thus they became burgesses of Leicester in the very fullest sense of the word. As the next century progressed the membership grew, and soon

[1] "Robert, Count of Meulan to Ralph the Butler and all his men, French as well as English of all his land of England, greeting. Know ye that I have granted to my merchants of Leicester the gild of their merchants with all the customs by which they held in the time of King William, and of King William, his son, and now in the time of King Henry." This grant is dated between 1103-1118. Bateson, *Records*, vol. I, p. I.

[2] The first roll gives practically nothing but the names of those who enter the gild and their payments. Their names, however, often indicate their occupation, and show that not alone the merchant, sometimes designated by the French form "marchant," enrolled himself within the gild membership, but the dyer, the weaver, the tailor, the shearman, the shoemaker, the cook, the pistor, the stabler, all were admitted. This roll corroborates Professor Gross's contention that craftsmen were freely admitted to the gild merchant. *Op. cit.*, vol. i, p. 107. For the roll see Bateson, *op. cit.*, vol. i, p. 12 *et seq.* Professor Ashley, in his criticism of Gross's *Gild Merchant*, enters into an elaborate discussion, disputing this fact. *Historic Surveys*, p. 216.

the gild developed a mechanism which enabled it to assume control of the financial as well as industrial affairs of the borough. With a definite meeting place—the gild hall—and regularly elected officers, gild meetings became important centres of burghal activity. By 1258, the presiding officer was known as the mayor.[1] As the chief civic official he dispensed funds collected for town purposes at gild meetings. He presided over the gild court, where in accordance with gild regulations infringement of gild law met its merited punishment. The gild merchant of Leicester had developed far.

But among the entries in the gild rolls for 1260 may be found an interesting item relating how some gild members, significantly weavers and fullers, at a general meeting held that year agreed to some regulations there made for their industry, and at the same time promised not to hold any further "morningspeech" except in the presence of two of the merchants of the gild. Five years later the rolls tell how the weavers had made certain rules for their craft by themselves, and as the record has it, "against the community of the gild merchants." Later still, in 1275, the mayor in a fully attended gild session, accused certain fullers of holding a "morningspeech" without the presence of the "jurats" commanded by the gild community.[2] What is the significance of entries such as these upon gild merchant rolls? Why must members who were subject to gild rules promise not to hold meetings apart from gild meetings, nor to make regulations for themselves which the gild merchant considered detrimental to its "community?" Is it not clear that these craftsmen, especially the weavers and fullers,

[1] Bateson, *op. cit.*, vol. i, p. 75.

[2] Bateson, *Records*, vol. i, pp. 89, 108, 168.

were beginning to feel the need of some closer union where they as men most directly interested in their particular craft might make rules they deemed necessary for themselves, free from the oversight and direction of the gild merchant?

Unfortunately the Leicester rolls do not disclose the whole story of the transition movement, of the gradual withdrawal of gild artisans, group by group, from the gild merchant's control. They do not show the period at which, the weavers and fullers apparently in the lead, they broke away entirely from the parent union, the merchant gild, to form closer associations of their own. In 1343, the gild merchant was still making regulations for the fullers, insisting that they carry on their work "as was of old appointed."[1] But the last gild merchant roll extant is significant in this connection. By that time, 1380, the gild merchant had evidently become nothing more than a mechanism for enrolling the names of those who desired to become burgesses of Leicester.[2] The roll no longer registers rules for the conduct of the borough's industrial affairs, nor shows disbursement of gild funds. There is no allusion to trials for the redress and punishment of offences against gild law. There is nothing but lists of names of newly-admitted burgesses. The Leicester gild merchant as the organ which had controlled borough trade and industry was no more, and its disappearance presupposes the success of its rivals, those unions of special crafts which had deserted the parent gild and assumed charge each of its individual interests. Not altogether at their own discretion, however, for a year before, in 1379,[3] because of "falsity which people talk and speak of," in the weavers' craft, the town had elected two weavers to institute search for defective work in their

[1] Bateson, *Records*, vol. ii, p. 50. [2] *Ibid.*, p. 196. [3] *Ibid.*, p. 195.

own trade, and to present offenders to the town authorities. The latter also took upon themselves to forbid the formation of associations of craftsmen when they considered them detrimental to the interest of the community.[1] We do not know when the existence of craft gilds was really sanctioned within Leicester. Fully a century passes before the town records show the presence of any such organizations.

Perhaps the very fact that after 1380 no minutes of the proceedings of the gild merchant are preserved has a special significance. The gild could not be expected to register its own downfall, at least not consciously. Even its officers had probably withdrawn into one of the rising craft gilds, so that no one was left to record the last acts in its history.

We have, however, seen enough to account at least for the rise of the weavers' and fullers' gilds in Leicester as a direct outgrowth of the gild merchant. The relation between the gild merchant and the incipient craft gilds there was apparently something as follows: Craftsmen of all kinds were from the first freely admitted into the gild merchant, subject like all other members by pledge and the payment of the entrance fee to its regulations and oversight. Thus they must have been equally interested in upholding the authority of that organization for a time at least. With the increase in numbers of artisans interested in a particular industry, however, those dwelling probably in the same neighborhood, drawn together at first in social intercourse, where business interests in

[1] *Ibid.*, p. 197. "It is agreed and ordained that henceforth the 'lochelmen' called watermen shall be separated and shall serve the commune well and loyally according to the custom before used and if any association be found among them and they shall be attainted of this, that the chamberlains cause 3s., 4d. to be levied from each of them, at the first default, to the use and profit of the community."

time naturally came in for a share of discussion, felt the need of a closer union to further these interests. It was then but natural that they should get together to make rules more in keeping with their own ideas for the management of their particular trade. As members still of the gild merchant, these artisans would naturally at first keep such rules secret from the merchants as a whole. It is equally natural that when officials or members of the gild merchant in the conduct of their trade discovered such rulings among the artisans, they should report what they considered breaches of gild regulations to the proper tribunal, namely, the gild merchant, which at the appointed time and place would take cognizance of such dereliction, and seek to prevent a repetition of the same offence. This much the Leicester records clearly show.

That the parent association should have objected at first to any infringement of its rules, and later to a withdrawal of its former members, is a perfectly natural situation. Just what form such objection assumed in Leicester or in any other English borough we have as yet no means of determining. Whether any decided upheaval occurred or not we do not know, nor on the other hand can we assert with Hibbert,[1] that the gild merchant was glad to depute its powers, as division of labor developed, and to exercise its functions through smaller and specialized agents. The evidence in the Leicester rolls would indicate that the parent gild asserted its rights over its members just as long as possible. Furthermore, if our conception of the gild merchant as the association of burgesses for the monopoly and control of their municipal trade and toll be correct, that body would in any town naturally resent an infringement upon its rights and privileges. Enrollment, therefore, of particu-

[1] *Influence and Development of English Gilds*, pp. 20, 21.

lar craftsmen in any separate organizations would necessitate withdrawal from the larger union. This theory is opposed to that heretofore advocated by writers upon craft gilds who maintain that many of the burgesses were enrolled in unions of their own while still members of the gild merchant.[1] But it seems more probable that formal enrollment in an established craft gild early pre-

[1] Professor Gross maintains that even after craftsmen had united they still remained in the common gild merchant (*Gild Merchant*, vol. i, p. 115), and that for some time after certain of them were united, regulations were probably made for them by that organization. (Note 1, p. 116.) The examples cited in support of this assertion, however, really contain no proof of membership in the two species of gilds at the same time. Mr. Gross makes no distinction here between the gild merchant's exercise of its earliest powers, when, before the rise of craft gilds, it naturally made regulations for the interests of artisan members who had no separate organizations, and the position it occupied in its decadence. He quotes, for examples, the part played by the gild merchant in Andover in the thirteenth century and in Worcester two centuries later. Yet when we find the Worcester "yeld marchaunt" of the fifteenth century making ordinances for the regulation of various borough affairs, it is acting not as an early gild merchant, but as a general town assembly where articles were made by the "hole assent of the citesens inhabitantes" and proclaimed as town custom "at every law day." See Smith, *Eng. Gilds*, p. 376. The same criticism of confusion of date and function applies to Professor Cunningham's citation of conditions in Beverley. He states upon Poulson's authority that "another regulation of this gilda mercatoria or merchant fraternity was appointing lesser gilds with an alderman or warden to each." *Growth of Eng. Ind.*, vol. 1, p. 310. The evidence in the *Beverley Town Documents* does not warrant this statement. Moreover, Mr. Leach directly refutes it. *Beverley Town Doc.*, Introd. xli; see, also, p. 74. Professor Seligman (*op. cit.*, p. 57) holds a similar view of simultaneous membership, and to substantiate it quotes the Dublin Gild Merchant Roll of 1226. But there is nothing there to show that craft gild members were found enrolled in the gild merchant of that city. All that this Dublin Roll can be made to prove is that men of every known trade were admitted to membership in the gild merchant. It thus corroborates the evidence presented by the Leicester Rolls of the same period. See *Historic and Municipal Documents of Ireland*, vol. i, p. 82, for the Dublin Roll.

cluded any idea of a like relation with the parent association. This at least holds true so long as the gild merchant continued to exercise the function for which it was originally created.

It would be interesting to know the duration of the transition stage between the rise of craft gilds and the end of the gild merchant; to ascertain, for instance, whether the craftsmen withdrew gradually, group by group, or whether upon the desertion of one or two craft unions the entire gild merchant organization disbanded. Not only is the absence of any record of the break-up of the gild merchant significant, but the fact that the newly-rising craft gilds left no trace of their beginnings suggests an interpretation. Just as the parent union would not be apt to record its own downfall, the newly-forming associations would not at first be in a position to record their rise. Indeed it is a fact worthy of consideration that when records of craft gilds emerge in the later thirteenth and fourteenth centuries, the mere appearance of the records is indicative of a change in borough conditions. By that time a representative body of townsmen had taken charge of borough government, assuming control of all financial and industrial administration within their respective borders. The old gild merchant was here superseded by town authority and the registration of industrial affairs transferred to borough records. That is in fact the place where traces of the next stage in craft-gild development are to be found.

Interesting evidence of craft development has been offered by the recent publication of the Bristol town records. In the later Middle Ages Bristol ranked probably as second in importance of English boroughs.[1]

[1] Next to London, Bristol was the first town to acquire the dignity of a county in England. *Little Red Book*, vol. i, Introd., xii.

Albeit no rolls of the gild merchant are to be found among the papers yet published, there is proof that the institution early existed in Bristol,[1] and that as late as 1314 it was exercising some of its functions.[2] In the time of John, moreover, the Bristol burgesses were allowed "all reasonable gilds," as they had had them before his day.[3] The exact nature of these "reasonable gilds" does not appear, and it is almost the middle of the fourteenth century before it can truly be said that craft gilds were an established institution in the borough. By that time Bristol had a representative municipal body,[4] and to the efforts of one of its officials we owe the record of this second stage in craft-gild development.[5] In 1346 Bristol craftsmen were already drawn together into different groups concerned in the development of particular trades. To further their interests these men on various occasions presented themselves before the city authorities for the sanction and approval of regulations which had

[1] From a fourteenth century Inquisition into the rights of the town, it seems that the Mayor, Bailiffs and Commonalty and their ancestors claimed to have had a free merchant gild and all things thereto pertaining. *Ibid.*, xx.

[2] An extant record of Bristol Customs, of this date, shows that from the "profits of the Gild of Merchants and of the town" various town works were supported. Gross, *op. cit.*, vol. ii, p. 25.

[3] *Little Red Book*, vol. i, Introd., xiii.

[4] In the rolls of John Bristol was one of the towns recorded as having a mayor, which symbolized the "communa." Stubbs, *Constit. Hist.*, vol. iii, pp. 561, 559.

[5] The Recorder of the city at that time had caused all the ordinances, customs and liberties of the town to be registered. *Little Red Book*, vol. i, Introd., xxi. Indeed the wealth of material for craft-gild development contained in this *Little Red Book*, published in 1900, amply justifies the indignation felt and expressed by Toulmin Smith when in 1868 he was refused access to the corporation records of Bristol. See *Eng. Gilds*, Note, p. 283.

been drawn up for the government of their respective trades. From time to time as new needs made themselves felt this same method of procedure was continued, and the character of the additional privileges from time to time allowed these craftsmen suggests the line of development of craft organization.

Taking one of these Bristol crafts as an example, we have an interesting picture of the development of a gild. That of the barbers is first mentioned in 1395,[1] when a number of men, thirteen in all, "assembled for the government of their craft," appeared before the "mayor, sheriff and the forty men" who "have rule of the town by virtue of the charter of liberty of Lord Edward, late King of England." There, in the presence of both town authorities and craftsmen, certain rules for the guidance of the barber's trade were recorded. These were neither very important nor very numerous. But when next they presented themselves before the municipality, in 1418,[2] they were in need of more stringent regulations and a better organization. To provide for a proper oversight of the barbers' craft, they asked permission to elect annually two searchers, who should be sworn before the mayor; and to prevent encroachments on their monopoly from men of other trades, they asked that an apprenticeship of seven years be made requisite for any one thereafter serving as a barber within the city, and that such a requirement have a place among their ordinances. They asked that this be done to avert the destruction which they saw impending over their craft unless "they have remedy and be succored and supported" by the "very wise discretions" of the town officers.

Fortunately for us, inasmuch as we are thus enabled to

[1] *Little Red Book*, vol. ii, p. 69. [2] *Ibid.*, p. 135.

watch the process of gild organization, this barber's craft is late in forming an association. But many of the numerous Bristol artisans appear to have been fully organized by the middle of the fourteenth century, as we shall observe later. The same movement was probably going on in most of the other important English boroughs. It had begun in London probably a century earlier. There by Henry III's time had been formed the cordwainers' gild.[1] Its ordinances at that time were made with the consent, indeed at the wish, of the mayor and other "barons" of the city to suppress deceptive practices then known to be in use among the craftsmen. By 1303 it was felt that those earlier regulations had not accomplished their purpose, and the city authorities ordained the appointment of four reputable men to institute a search at least once a month for the detection of articles made in contravention of the cordwainers' ordinances.[2] The same need of supervision is apparent in the cappers' craft,[3] as well as in the lorimers'. The latter indeed went so far as to reward the mayor for his share in helping on the craft organization with a product of their skill in the shape of a "becoming bridle."[4]

While the gap in the Leicester records between the rise of craft gilds and the break-up of the gild merchant is not bridged by the Bristol account, yet enough is given to make it perfectly apparent what power had asserted itself over the newly rising craft gilds. By the middle of the fourteenth century the mayor and his fellow-officers held sway over all trade organizations in Bristol. The gild merchant by that time had completely

[1] *Liber Albus*, appendix ii, p. 441.

[2] *Liber Custumarum*, Introd., lxix.

[3] *Ibid.*, Introd., lxxi.

[4] *Liber Cust.*, Introd., lix.

disappeared and its industrial successors, the craft gilds, were entirely submissive to municipal control.

This recognition of, and submission to, municipal authority characteristic of these associations established by burghal authority during this period are features likewise of similar associations chartered by the crown. For illustration we may trace the evolution within one of the boroughs of an early trade gild which by royal permission enjoyed industrial freedom in its own sphere. We have already seen that, although Oxford had already been granted the privilege of a gild merchant,[1] probably in the time of Henry I, bodies of special artisans, the weavers and cordwainers, had also purchased the right to have associations as early at least as the thirty-first year of the same monarch.[2] We have moreover found this union of Oxford weavers among those early artisan gilds which were excluded by their fellow-townsmen from enjoying the usual privileges of citizens. This hostility must have continued throughout the thirteenth century, since Exchequer records of the ninth year of Henry III show a payment by the Oxford weavers for a writ commanding the mayor and provosts of that borough to allow them to enjoy the liberties which they had had in the time of Henry II.[3] How effective this royal command proved in restraining the opposition of the Oxford authorities we have no means of knowing, but restrictions were probably still applied to the weavers, for in the early years of Edward I they had become so reduced

[1] *Supra*, p. 14.

[2] *Supra*, pp. 17-18.

[3] "The Weavers of Oxford fined in a Cask of Wine to have a Writ commanding the Mayor and Provosts of Oxford to let them have the same liberties in that Town, as well in Clothworking as in other Things which they had in the times of K. Henry II," . . . Madox, *Exchequer*, vol. i, p. 414.

in numbers and so decayed in fortune that that monarch, to relieve their distress, reduced the amount of the contribution they had annually made to his Exchequer, commanding that thereafter the sum be rendered " by the hand of the mayors and bailiffs of Oxford.[1]

In all probability this account represents the process by which the earliest craft gilds were brought under municipal control. It was not until the gilds and the town authorities came to terms that satisfactory conditions reigned in English boroughs. This view of the course of development is confirmed by the history of the London weavers.[2] They too had from the earliest times enjoyed the liberty of a gild. That they took full advantage of their privileges is evident from the fact that in the time of John and the establishment of the London commune,[3] the weavers' gild had become so obnox-

[1] *Ibid.*, p. 338, for the account of these Oxford weavers.

[2] No trace of a London gild merchant has as yet been found. Professor Gross thinks that such an institution was there dispensed with, because the rapid economic growth probably produced a net-work of craft gilds earlier than elsewhere. *Gild Merchant*, vol. i, p. 116, note. In 1132, however, there seems to be mention of a London "gialla," *i. e.*, gild hall, which measured fifty-two feet in width and one hundred and thirty-two feet in length. Bateson, *Mediaeval England*, p. 131. Did not this symbolize for London merchants what it did for those of other English boroughs, namely, their right to have a gild merchant? Recently there has come to light a London charter, drawn up apparently in the thirteenth century to confer citizenship upon a Florentine merchant, in which there is allusion to a London gild merchant. Nevertheless, Mr. C. G. Crump, who presents the bit of evidence, questions its conclusiveness as proof of the existence of that institution in London. He imagines that a "chancery clerk endeavoring to draft a charter to convert a Florentine merchant into a citizen of London might well have thought fit to mention a gild merchant as a matter of common form, even if none actually existed." *Eng. Hist. Review*, vol. xviii, p. 315.

[3] Norton, *Commentaries*, p. 315.

ious that the city offered the king an inducement more substantial than the gild was in the habit of making to prevail upon that monarch to order the union abolished entirely.[1] The records show that the citizens of London made good their promises of payment but failed to effect their end. The weavers' gild continued to flourish, and the contest waged fiercely between it and the city authorities, until the twenty-eighth year of Edward I. Then, for some aggression probably more daring than usual the weavers were summoned to appear before the mayor to answer a charge of violating their own early ordinances and of establishing new regulations "of their own authority in prejudice of all the commonalty."[2] The weavers at this time were apparently impressed with the weightier authority of the powers in command. They pleaded "guilty," praying to be allowed "ordinances for all time to be holden," infringement whereof to be duly punished "according to the ordinances of the mayor of London."[3]

Conditions such as these indicate clearly the change taking place in community life. With the decline of the gild merchant and the removal of its authority over industrial relations there would have been no check upon the rising craft organizations if the municipality had not brought them under its control. Nor would the craft gilds have alone been able to carry out the rules which

[1] Madox, *op. cit.*, vol. i, p. 405. [2] *Liber Cust.*, p. 121, 126.

[3] The earliest extant charter to the London weavers is significant in this connection. It conceded that they might hold their gild "with all the franchises and customs which they had in the time of King Henry" his grandfather; that no one should interfere with their craft in the city or in Southwark or elsewhere, unless belonging to their gild. It also forbade any one doing them "injury or contumely" under penalty. This is the charter granted probably by Henry I, some time between 1162–1171. *Ibid.*, Introd., lx., p. 33.

from time to time they enacted to control their respective trades. The interests of the gilds as well as of the community were best served by coöperation. Not that either recognized the advantage of mutual concessions at once. In the case of the early crown-chartered gilds especially, repeated conflicts and considerable experience were needed to force those associations to yield the proper respect to the greater power inherent in civic authorities and to bring them thus into any semblance of submission. Although as we have seen the London weavers appeared to submit, yet from later indications it is clear that another period of aggression on the part of that gild and of more rigorous protest from the municipal body were required to establish anything like harmony between those two factions.

Herein lies doubtless the true understanding of the change which took place in town and craft administration. The decay of the gild merchant and the advance of the representative municipal government must have been closely related phenomena, in the progress of which the newly rising craft gilds played their part. Indeed theirs was perhaps the principal part, since their withdrawal from the gild merchant was responsible for the break-up of the latter, as the Leicester records have disclosed. In boroughs such as Bristol with a prosperous commercial life and numberless craftsmen who would not be slow to see the advantage of individual unions, the gild merchant early yielded its place and powers to the commune established there in the time of John, and to the rising craft gilds. The older system would inevitably become unwieldy with the rapid development of trades and would therefore no longer be capable of performing its functions satisfactorily in a progressive community.

The burgesses in their petition to the crown for rights of self-government which resulted in their recognition as a commune were hastening the decline of the gild merchant. In the earlier period they had petitioned for the privilege of the institution they were now outgrowing. At that time it seemed the best machinery for the advancement of their trade interests. Now, however, with the right to elect municipal officers from among themselves to assume charge not only of the town's industrial and financial business but of its administrative and judicial affairs as well, they realized that community interests as a whole should be controlled by the commune, the representative municipal organization. The officers who had formerly presided over the gild merchant now held their sessions in the mayor's court. There rather than at the gild court were craft-gild officials sworn in, craft by-laws read, discussed and either ratified or disallowed, before enrollment among the borough proceedings. There, too, as ordered by borough proclamation, offenders against craft rules were brought for judgment. At this stage, consequently, craft gilds were municipal undertakings dependent upon civic authority for whatever powers they exercised—indeed for their very existence.

By the middle of the fourteenth century municipal development, due hitherto to enlarging industrial life among the separate towns, was becoming more and more dependent on the expansion of the nation's economic ambitions. While local diligence had so far been responsible for the development of borough trade and industry, national support of the country's mercantile interests was beginning to promise results farther-reaching than municipal ambitions, bounded by local limits, would or could contemplate or attain. That feeling of contempt for trade expressed in the thirteenth century must largely have passed away before the end of Edward III's reign. By that time not only were craft gilds fully established under municipal domination, but they were filling so important a place as organs for the supervision of the methods of manufacture and of trade that a statute directs that "artificers and men of mysteries shall each choose his own mystery before the next Candlemas, and having so chosen it, he shall henceforth use no other."[1] Membership in a craft gild was thus an obligation established by the state, the king himself setting the example by enrolling himself in the ranks.[2] It was, doubtless, Edward's recognition of their importance as national benefactors which led him to bestow so freely upon the greater London companies that series of royal charters by which the livery companies became an established feature of London, and thus of national industrial life.

With such prestige it was an easy matter for craft gilds as they grew in wealth and numbers to gain increasing privileges, and as bodies exercising national as well as local influence, to enter upon the career of power spreading out before them. Both national and municipal government were earnestly engaged in enlarging and developing England's mercantile resources, and, with these, craft interests were directly concerned. Thus the gilds or mysteries, as they began to be termed, under the leadership of the London companies, enjoyed a most prosperous period. They employed the powers and privileges they possessed to the fullest extent, usurping greater ones when they could, at once dominating and being dominated by

[1] 37 Edward III, c. 6.

[2] That monarch became a member of the Linen-armourers, later known as the Merchant Taylors. Herbert, *Twelve Great Livery Companies*, vol. i, p. 28.

both state and municipality, now encouraged and again made to atone for transgression by the powers above them, enjoying to the full the license which the system in its perfected state was able to provide. To the uninitiated, however, to the great public, their privileged position seemed based upon an infringement of the Englishman's natural rights, and their power an occasion for abuse which needed to be curbed and restrained.

As a result of this conflict of forces we have the English industrial life of the fifteenth and sixteenth centuries, in which an apparent contradiction is evident in the state's policy toward craft gilds. On the one hand, it fostered, encouraged and enlarged their powers; on the other, brought to a sense of craft aggression, it attempted to check the evils of monopoly and of license. A series of statutes beginning in the time of Henry VI was continued by successive governments, until the famous Elizabethan Statute of Apprentices supposedly brought order into the industrial world, though it sounded the death-knell of these all-powerful and ubiquitous industrial giants. The state, apparently, no longer took their interests into account in its scheme of economic control, but ruthlessly intruding upon their management of craft concerns, deprived them of both duties and privileges.

How far, however, this legislation can be regarded as the outcome of deliberate hostility on the part of the English government, and how far it acted as a factor in the decline of the gild system, are interesting questions worthy of a more extended consideration.

CHAPTER I

POLICY OF THE GOVERNMENT WITH REFERENCE TO CRAFT GILDS

THE foregoing account of the rise of the gild system serves to show that by the middle of the fourteenth century craft organizations were well-marked features of England's industrial life, playing constantly a more and more important part in the development of burghal interests and ambitions. The fourteenth century was a period of rapid development and in dealing with it, it is necessary to take into consideration both social and political forces, with their corresponding influences upon economic conditions. The social disturbance caused by the Black Death in 1348 brought into sharp contrast decaying feudal customs and rising modern ideals, and necessitated increased national as well as local effort to control and direct the energies concerned in the conflict.

Politically, the beginning of the great war with France involved England in Continental relations, which brought in their train new influences to react upon her social and industrial structure. Contact with neighboring peoples, with their older and more complex civilization, brought about an ardent appreciation of the luxury they enjoyed and created new desires, which could be met only by the introduction of foreign artisans. The immigration of these into England was thereafter encouraged as a deliberate part of the national policy of Edward III. The duties and obligations which thereby devolved upon national and local governments required a broader conception of responsibility to both native and foreign-born subject. Place and protection had to be provided for the stranger invited to England, an undertaking at that time rendered doubly difficult because of the jealousy constantly shown by craft associations already established, which became increasingly aggressive at this wholesale introduction of foreign artisans, menacing the material interests of English gildsmen. To meet its new obligations and satisfy its growing ambitions for national power, the national executive was compelled to assume a greater part in the regulation of the nation's social and industrial forces. This policy demanded a more rigid system of general social control, such as the state proceeded to set in motion by various means within its power. In every department of state royal proclamation and statutory enactment were brought into requisition to announce the government's will.

Beginning of Government Intervention in Craft Gild Concerns.

1. *Action of 1388.*—In keeping with the general policy thus outlined, the English government in 1388 turned its attention to the gild system within the realm. Desiring, apparently, detailed information concerning that system,[1] it sent writs throughout the shires of the country calling upon sheriffs to proclaim within their jurisdiction that masters, wardens and overlookers of all the mysteries

[1] Writs were sent out also for returns from the social gilds. The fact is worthy of notice that, whereas craft gilds were merely asked for "their charters or letters patent where they had any," social gilds were to give details as to the form and authority of their foundation, the manner of their oaths, gatherings, liberties, privileges, ordinances, lands, tenements, rents and possessions. Smith, *English Gilds*, p. 127.

and crafts that held charters or letters patent of the king or of his predecessors were to bring them before the king and his council, for "certain good and reasonable causes" brought to the royal knowledge at a previous Parliament.

Unfortunately records do not divulge the nature of these "reasonable causes," and writers in their efforts to explain governmental action at this time have had to supply the deficiency as best they could. A wide field is thus open for speculation. From the returns sent in by the social gilds in response to the writs addressed to them at this time it is easy to divine the interpretation they placed upon the crown's measure. They evidently considered it the outcome of a desire for an account of their worldly wealth, for first in their returns they placed information regarding the property they held.[1] This same understanding of the government's motive is apparent in the only extant record of a return sent in by a craft gild.[2] The officers of the barbers of London, replying to the writ addressed to them, certified to the council "the form, manner and condition of all the articles, customs and their circumstances," adding, "the which Company have neither tenements nor rents to their common use." The latter clause is suggestive, for as a craft gild they had not been required to make such a report.

But the motive, whatever it may be, has no real bearing upon the object of this investigation.[3] It is mainly of

[1] The peltyers and the tailors' gilds of Norwich in spite of their craft names seem from their ordinances to have been social gilds, and sent in their returns as such. Smith, *op. cit.*, pp. 28–34.

[2] *Annals of the Barber-Surgeons*, p. 32.

[3] Miss Bateson, in her Introduction to the *Cambridge Gild Records*, xxviii (published in 1903) assumes that the primary purpose of the inquiry was to find out how far it might be necessary to put a stop to the licensing of further mortmains. As a direct result, accord-

interest to know that craft gilds were a well established part of the gild system of the realm[1] at this time, and a most important one, to judge from the constant mention of them in statute book and town muniments, and from the traces which still exist in their own "ordinals." London, then as always the leader in the English commercial world, furnishes the earliest material for an inquiry into the working of the system. There craft gilds had been fostered, encouraged, even called into existence at least as early as the time of Edward III. The practice of granting crown charters to these London gilds began in the twelfth century and continued throughout the thirteenth and fourteenth,[2] and reached a culminating point when Edward by his liberal encouragement of the more important associations made possible the position assumed by the livery companies of his day.

The practice of issuing crown charters for craft gilds seems however at this epoch to have been confined to the London gilds. In Bristol, where, as we have seen, craft gilds were exceedingly numerous by this time, no such chartered privileges are recorded. There the crafts sought municipal authority for any privileges they deemed necessary;[3] and the meekness with which they apparently

ing to her views, 15 Rich. II, c. 5, was enacted, and the action of Henry VIII in dissolving religious fraternities was here foreshadowed. Professor Ashley sees an additional reason in a dislike for journeymen's associations which were attempting to shelter themselves under cover of religious gilds. *Eng. Econ. Hist.*, vol. ii, p. 137.

[1] The original writs sent out at this time are still extant in some of the shires in different sections of the country. Smith, *op. cit.*, p. 132, note.

[2] Edward I had also chartered a few companies, besides confirming some earlier chartered grants. Herbert, *op. cit.*, vol. i, p. 26.

[3] Apparently the first record of a royal charter to a Bristol craft gild is that granted the tailors in 1399. *Archæological Journal*, 1881, p. 113.

approached their city officials testifies to their recognition of, and acquiescence in, municipal control.[1] This attitude is doubtless responsible for the smoothness with which that borough's industrial affairs were then conducted,[2] a characteristic not always true of London nor probably of other English towns. Municipalities usually disapproved of crown charters to craft gilds. Indeed they regarded a too liberal grant of power to the crafts as wholly dangerous, and finally voiced their grievances in a petition directed to Parliament in 1376. Therein they complained that many mayors and bailiffs of boroughs within the realm were hindered from performing what they considered their duty in craft matters because of special charters granted certain mysteries. They went on to ask that such charters be repealed, and that no more like them be granted in the future, in order that municipal officials might not be "restrained from the due corrections pertaining to their offices."[3]

Gild opposition to the power exercised by civic authorities occasionally reached during this century considerable strength. We find, for instance, one of the social gilds apparently struggling to retain its early democratic ideals, and actually objecting to the admission of either mayors or bailiffs into membership.[4] But

[1] Volume ii of the *Little Red Book* is filled with examples.

[2] Hunt, Bristol's historian, who seems to have had access to the "Great Red Book" of the corporation, shows how this bond between the civic authorities and the craft gilds was rendered necessary by the disorganization which prevailed within that city after the desolations of the Black Death, and that the trade interests in which both town and crafts were directly concerned drew those bodies into harmonious relations. *Bristol* (*Historic Towns*), pp. 79, 80.

[3] There is no record of a response being accorded this petition. *Rotuli Parliamentorum*, vol. ii, p. 331.

[4] In Lincoln, in 1350, mayors or bailiffs were not welcome in the

in general both gild members and townsmen paid tribute to the authority they recognized as inherent in the office of mayor. A neglect on the part of that official to enforce even municipal regulations against the gilds evoked, sometimes at least, the public disapproval which found such forceful expression on one occasion at Coventry.[1]

Notwithstanding rare outbursts such as these from indignant human nature, it would seem that, on the whole, by the middle of the fourteenth century municipal authorities were making good their claim to consideration as the power in control of trade interests within their respective boundaries, and also that for the most part the relations existing between them and the craft gilds of their various localities were fairly harmonious. This seems at least to have become true in the main for London as well as for Bristol. In Norwich, as we shall see, a longer period of stress was needed to bring about this same result. The length of time consumed in individual towns in establishing such harmonious relations probably varied with the importance of the industrial interests at stake.

But whatever the source of craft-gild power, whether royal favor or merely municipal authority, the gilds seem all alike to have made good use of their opportunities, such as they were. In the industrial activity of the times, moreover, these opportunities were constantly increasing as trade and manufactures, stimulated by government encouragement and protection, rose, developed and ex-

gilds, "being founded by people of the common and middling sort; and if they be admitted they shall keep their proper place and not thrust themselves too forward." Lambert, *Two Thousand Years of Gild Life*, p. 107.

[1] In 1387, the commons rose and threw loaves of bread at the mayor's head in St. Mary's Hall, because he did not punish the bakers who "kept not the assize." *Eng. Hist. Rev.*, vol. ix, p. 635.

panded. As the organs directly concerned in this mercantile prosperity, steadily receiving or usurping privileges to keep pace with their growing strength, it was no wonder that before the middle of the fifteenth century, craft gilds by their aggression should have called for governmental intervention.

2. *Act of Henry VI, 1437.*—Complaints against craft gilds and their methods must have become general when in 1437 the commons petitioned Parliament to take matters into its hands, because

> masters, wardens and people of the gilds, fraternities and other companies incorporate, often times by colour of rule and governance and other terms in general words to them granted and confirmed by charters and letters patent of the king's progenitors, make among themselves many unlawful and unreasonable ordinances, as well of such things whereof the cognizance, punishment and correction all only pertaineth to the King, Lords of Franchises and other persons, and whereby our Sovereign Lord, the King and others be disherited of their profits and franchises as of things which oftentimes in confederacy is made for their singular profit and common damage to the people.

In response to this petition it was enacted that in the future officers of such companies should "cause all their letters patent and charters to be registered of record before the justices of the peace in the counties or the chief governors of the said cities, boroughs and towns where such gilds be." Likewise, that thereafter no ordinances which might be considered harmful were to be enforced unless first approved as lawful or reasonable by the aforesaid authorities and recorded by them.[1]

[1] 15 Henry VI, c. 6; *Rot. Parl.*, vol. iv, p. 507, registers the answer given the petition. "Be it as it is desired . . . as long as it shall like the Kyng."

Although the statute thus charges craft gilds with framing "unlawful ordinances," yet the lack of any specification of the nature of their unlawfulness has given writers who desire to determine the cause of this enactment free scope here also for conjecture. Professor Cunningham, reviewing conditions of the previous century, when, as he says, the monopolistic tendencies of the craft gilds were very pronounced, reminds us of the troubles arising between the London municipality and the weavers in 1321,[1] the difficulties which evoked the petition of the mayors to Parliament in 1376,[2] and enumerates certain obnoxious practices of the fishmongers and vintners in that city. He then proceeds to say that in 1437 the charges became more specific, although based still upon the same general ground of complaint, namely, that the gilds set the local authorities at defiance and so injured the public. Hence this act of Henry VI,[3] with its proposed remedy, approval and registry of gild ordinances before the justices of the peace.[4]

By this interpretation we are given to understand that a decided change of policy had been inaugurated. Since craft gilds had been making unlawful ordinances, henceforth they were to submit all by-laws to justices of the peace for approval and registration before they could put them into execution. Yet what had been the procedure heretofore employed by those organizations in making new by-

[1] *Growth of Eng. Ind. and Commerce*, vol. i, p. 397.

[2] *Supra*, p. 43.

[3] Professor Cunningham quotes as a part of this statute, after the charge of "unlawful ordinances" another clause, "as well in prices of wares," but this latter accusation has no place in the statute of Henry VI, as found upon the statute book.

[4] Here he stops short of the actual wording. Approval is to be obtained from the justices of the peace in the counties, or from the chief governors of the cities and towns where the gilds were located.

laws effective? Was the method thus outlined a departure from the former custom? Can we admit after the survey thus far made, that the gilds could be accused at this stage of their development of setting local authorities at defiance in the text of their ordinances? Is the point here emphasized, namely, the approval of the justices of the peace, the true remedy intended by the act? It must be apparent that craft organizations everywhere, whether founded upon municipal or royal grants of privilege, had been brought by this time into subjection to the developing power of the commune. Craft gilds had as we have seen been bringing their by-laws for sanction before the representatives of the civic body for many years, so that approval and registry of craft ordinances were by no means novelties.

In fact a study of every accessible set of craft ordinances from the thirteenth century proves that it was not for lack of oversight by local authorities that the gilds had become thus defiant, to the injury of the public, in 1437. In London, as we have already noted, as early as Henry III's reign the by-laws of the lorimers received the assent of the mayors and "barons." Throughout that century city oversight and correction of craft ordinances are fully apparent. The same condition of affairs lasted throughout the fourteenth century, even in the troublesome weavers' gild. Not only were craft by-laws submitted to the city authorities for their approval, but the latter were in one case requested to command that those laws should be inviolably observed.[1] In Bristol we have also found the mayor and his colleagues in com-

[1] This provision is found among the vintners' by-laws of 1370. *Trans. London and Middlesex Archæological Society*, vol. iii, p. 416. Examples can be indefinitely multiplied. See Riley, *Memorials of London*.

plete control over craft gilds. Not only the dyers, the drapers, the barbers, the fullers and the cordwainers, but even the weavers,—one of the earlier type of artisan gilds perhaps, since their ordinances had been "in use of old," —were accustomed to amend their statutes and add new ones before the mayor.[1] Furthermore all craft ordinances recognized by the Bristol authorities in this and in the following centuries expressly state the reservation by the town officers of the right to amend any provision, if it be profitable to both town and craft.

In Norwich, which was at this time probably the third city of the realm,[2] control of the crafts seems to have been secured with more trouble for the municipality. Yet at the date of this act the same conditions prevailed here as elsewhere. In 1256, Henry III granted the citizens as one of their charter privileges that no gild or fraternity should be allowed in that city if it were considered "to its damage."[3] The Norwich authorities thenceforth took advantage of this royal gift to replenish their coffers with fines levied upon gilds defiant enough to disregard the the prohibition.[4] However, after some dire experiences, in which both town and crafts probably suffered, a compromise seems to have been effected in 1413, as a result of which citizenship and craft-gild membership came to

[1] *Little Red Book*, vol. ii, p. 4.

[2] In a list of contributions given by his chief boroughs in 1387 to Richard II, London is named first, Bristol second, and Norwich third. Quoted in Cunningham, *op. cit.*, vol. i, p. 341.

[3] Merewether and Stephens, *History of Boroughs*, p. 437. See, also, vol. 5 of Selden Soc. Pub. *Leet Jurisdiction in Norwich*, note in Introd., lxxxviii.

[4] In a Leet Roll of 21 Edward I, amercements appear "of the cobblers because they have a gild contrary to the prohibition of the lord king . . Of the saddlers because they likewise have a gild hurtful to the lord king. Of the fullers for the same." *Ibid.*

be identical terms.[1] Coventry, which since 1345[2] had been one of England's free and independent boroughs, privileged to manage its own municipal affairs, had by 1426 so far profited by its opportunities that its officials were in full control of the craft gilds within its territory. Nine years later, when the town authorities interfered to check deceptive practices among the ironworkers, they sternly commanded that "certain ordinances of the crafts be taken good heed to, lest the king's liege people should suffer thereby." They then provided of their own accord measures for the reformation of the ironworkers' trade.[3]

The state of affairs described in these four boroughs may safely be taken as typical of that existing elsewhere. With the exception of some belonging to the few craft companies with crown charters chiefly situated in London, not a single craft ordinance is to be found among all the records which does not show municipal authorization and approval.[4] It is certainly therefore not on account of failure to secure local approval of gild by-laws that this statute of Henry VI can be said to have been enacted.

Considering next the application of the provision emphasized by Professor Cunningham, that approval of craft

[1] There had been much turmoil over city elections. Other misfortunes, such as a disastrous fire and an exhausted treasury, seem to have been also instrumental in bringing the factions to terms. Blomefield, *History of the County of Norfolk*, vol. iii, p. 130.

[2] Harris, *Life in an Old English Town*, p. 106.

[3] *Ibid.*, p. 117. The corporation stated its idea of the duty inherent in its office, when it declared: "It is necessary and needful to every governor of city and town to see such rule and governance may be had by the which the king's people may be truly ruled and demened."

[4] Even in the charters granted to London crafts by Richard II, a certain right of the mayor over the gilds is distinctly acknowledged. This is also true of the charter granted the Bristol tailors.

ordinances should thenceforth be obtained from justices of the peace, we can discover no record which reveals a single set of craft by-laws ratified after 1437 by such a procedure. On the contrary, after the passage of this act, just as before, the policy of procuring municipal authorization was regularly continued. The conclusion, therefore, suggests itself either that this provision of the statute was wholly disregarded by craft bodies, or that the bearing of it has been wrongly construed.

A careful study of the wording of the entire enactment shows the interpretation is at fault, or at least that but part of the real state of affairs has been here made plain. The statute calls for approval and registry by the justices of the peace in the counties, or by the chief governors in the cities, boroughs or towns where such fraternities were located. Since records of craft gilds are found only in places where chief governors of some sort held sway, it seems warrantable to assert that the crafts were thoroughly obedient to the command of the statute. But so far as conditions in those cities, boroughs or towns were concerned, no change in existing methods of endorsement of craft ordinances was contemplated by this act of Henry VI. It merely confirmed, with the added authority of national legislation, a practice that had previously worked itself out in the principal boroughs of the country, where rising municipalities had brought craft gilds under their own control. All, therefore, that this act can be said to have accomplished was the strengthening of local administration in its supremacy over craft gilds.

However, granting for the present that Professor Cunningham's be the correct interpretation, and that this statute really intended to bring craft by-laws under the control of the justices of the peace, we are led to ask who filled the office of justices of the peace in England at this time, and why we do not find them confirming craft ordinances in accordance with the provision? Were they delinquent in the fulfilment of their duties?

Tracing the history of the institution of the office of justice of the peace in England, we find its foundation coincident with the social upheaval of the fourteenth century, when the government, to secure order throughout the realm, called these new guardians of public security into existence. A statute of the thirty-fourth year of Edward III first outlines the functions of the justice of the peace.[1] As the century advanced and the need of governmental regulation in all departments of state increased, the services of the justice of the peace as an administrative as well as judicial officer of the government were brought more and more into requisition. In the reign of Richard II the justice of the peace seems to be first mentioned as an official of a borough. His position there is of especial concern to our investigation. In compliance with the privileges accorded by crown charters to English towns, royal and county officials had been prohibited from exercising their duties within borough limits. Now the functions pertaining to the justice of the peace were introduced into borough administration, but for the discharge of them no new set of magistrates was created. The chief dignitaries of the town,

[1] 34 Edward III, c. i, provided that in every county of England there was to be appointed for the keeping of the peace, "one lord and with him three or four of the most worthy in the county, with some learned in the law, and they shall have power to restrain the offenders to take surety for good behavior hear and determine felonies and trespasses . . *etc.*" Since this investigation was made, a study of *The Office of Justice of the Peace in England in its Origin and Development*, by Charles Austin Beard, has been published by the Columbia University Press.

the mayor, recorder and aldermen, in addition to their ordinary duties, were to perform the work of the justices in the shires.

One of the earliest instances of this arrangement is furnished by a charter granted the city of York in the sixteenth year of Richard II, where the mayor and twelve aldermen are bidden to exercise the powers of justices of the peace.[1] The commission thus conferred upon York municipal authorities was repeated to others. Six years later it had been bestowed in Coventry,[2] and in accordance with English custom, a similar privilege was demanded by a sister borough, Nottingham.[3] The number of men deputed to bear the title of justice seems the only feature which varied in different places. York was allowed twelve justices, Nottingham four in addition to the mayor and recorder. Kingston-upon-Hull in Henry VI's time had its mayor and thirteen aldermen invested with the powers of justices. By this charter Kingston was created a county, separated from the county of York,

[1] Ashley, *Eng. Econ. Hist.*, vol. ii, p. 59, note 65, quoting from Drake's *Eboracum*, p. 206, "That the mayor and twelve aldermen of our city, and their successors; or four, three, or two of them with the said mayor, have full correction, *etc.*"

[2] Harris, *Life in an Old Eng. Town*, p. 98.

[3] Charter of Henry IV, dated Nov. 18, 1399, reads, "That they (Mayor, Bailiffs and Burgesses), and their heirs and successors, shall have for ever full correction, punishment, authority and power as fully and wholly as Justices of the Peace of labourers and of artificers have had or have exercised before this time in the county of Nottingham, to inquire, hear and determine by the Mayor and Recorder of the town aforesaid and four other upright and lawful men . . . to be selected by the Mayor . . . and that the aforesaid mayor . . . shall have all fines . . . arising from the same justiceship as fully as the Mayor, Bailiffs and Burgesses of the town of Coventry have obtained such fines . . . in the 22 year of the reign of Richard, the late king." *Nottingham Records*, vol. ii; p. 8.

and thus freed from the jurisdiction of Yorkshire magistrates.[1] Perhaps here lies the justification for the establishment of the justice of the peace as a borough official. As the more important boroughs were raised to the dignity of counties and separated from the surrounding districts, not only was the progress of municipal liberty advanced, but the position of the borough became defined in the national structure, and was confirmed by the legislation of succeeding centuries. A great similarity of function characterizes county and municipal magistrates. Both are called upon to hear and determine offenses against national enactments.[2]

But though borough officials had authority to act as justices of the peace, and although the act of 1437 according to Professor Cunningham, was intended to bring craft by-laws under the jurisdiction of those magistrates, yet from all accessible evidence after this legislative ruling as before, the same method of obtaining municipal endorsement was pursued by the craft gilds. In the simple capacity of borough officials do mayors and their brethren record their approval of gild ordinances. This is true in London three years after the passage of the act. The coopers[3] appeared before the mayor and aldermen, bringing a draft of certain provisions for the remedy of abuses which, in their opinion had "sclaundered the citee and gretly hindred the Crafte of Coupers." After reading the articles, and declaring them "consonant with

[1] Merewether and Stephens, *op. cit.*, pp. 859–866.

[2] Justices of the peace in the counties and mayors, *etc.*, in the cities, boroughs and towns were given equal powers in hearing and determining offenses. 2 Henry VI, c. 17. 11 Henry VI, c. 8, In the sixteenth century the same fact is apparent, as in 24 Henry VIII, c. 4; 5 Eliz., c. 4, sec. xxx.

[3] Firth, *Coopers Company*, p. 12.

reason," the civic authorities permitted them to be recorded, reserving to themselves power, however, to amend and correct the same. When the dyers of Bristol, in 1439,[1] required a new set of by-laws they addressed their petition to the municipal officials, "the worschipful and reverend Sirs, the Maire, Sherif, Baillifs and al the worthi men of the Commune Counsell of the towne of Bristow." The cordwainers, in 1443, and the pewterers in 1457, did likewise.

The policy of Henry VI was directed solely to strengthening municipal authority over craft gilds. This is well illustrated by the case of the Merchant Taylors of London. Henry had granted them a charter with great privileges, which the civic officials claimed were contrary to the liberties and customs of the city as recited in its charter. Appeal by the city for a repeal of the Merchant Taylors' charter brought from the king and council the command "to put in force all the articles of the great charter of the city notwithstanding the aforesaid charter of the tailors."[2] This same policy was displayed again in Reading. The king during a visit to that town had conferred an especial dignity upon the warden of the gild.[3] When, however, it was learned that this conflicted with the customs of the local authority, the abbot of the Reading

[1] *Little Red Book*, vol. ii, pp. 170, 176, 184.

[2] Clode, *Merchant Taylors*, p. 243.

[3] Reading was a mesne borough under an episcopal lord. The especial honor was permission to carry the mace before the king, which was a higher mark of authority than the Abbot permitted his own bailiff. When Henry VI in due time was informed that it was contrary to the franchises and liberties of the Monastery of Reading that "the Warden of the Gild bear in name or sign otherwise than as keeper of the Gild admitted by the Abbot," which was the two-tipped staves, the warden was warned "not to carry a mace, but only the two-tipped staves of the Abbot." Smith, *Eng. Gilds*. p. 298.

monastery, the honor was revoked, and the king was obliged to remind the gild warden that he was only the humble servant of the abbot, who with his bailiff was wholly supreme in that part of the world.

With the accession of Edward IV the customary method of securing municipal approval for craft regulations was for the most part continued. The pinners of London, in 1464, submitted their articles for the approbation of the mayor and corporation.[1] The clothworkers, successors to the earlier fullers and shearmen, when they wished to alter their by-laws did so with the advice of the mayor and aldermen.[2] But in the later policy of that monarch appears a tendency toward direct encouragement of the power of the crafts not to be overlooked in an attempt to outline the attitude of the English government toward craft gilds, a tendency which must, moreover, have stimulated the gilds themselves to greater audacity when their material interests were at stake.

In a charter of the seventh year of Edward IV to the London carpenters, after the usual grant of powers for a corporation, comes a statement that these craft masters and their commonalty are to make and enjoy their statutes at their pleasure, and to change them without impeachment either of the king, mayors or other officers of the crown, and that, moreover, all mayors, sheriffs and other officers are "to be intending, counselling and helping in all things" when their aid is so requested by the gild authorities.[3] The same rights, practically unrestrained, had been conferred upon the drapers of Shrewsbury in the very first year of Edward IV.[4] The London

[1] Gasquet, *Eve of the Reformation*, p. 368.

[2] Herbert, *Twelve Great Livery Companies*, vol. ii, p. 644.

[3] Jupp and Pocock, *Carpenters Company*, pp. 12–14.

[4] *Shropshire Archæological and Natural History Society Transactions*, 2d series, vol. viii, p. 180.

barbers had also obtained a similar gift of power, although in their charter the provision was inserted that their statutes or ordinances were not to be contrary to the laws and customs of the realm. Notwithstanding all this, it is interesting to note that in actual practice the barbers took good care to beseech the court of London aldermen for the ratification of their by-laws.[1]

Still another example of the same tendency is the lavish grant of privileges conferred upon the Exeter tailors—a memorable case in municipal and craft annals. In the early years of Edward IV, this craft obtained a very liberal charter in which, however, the king stated clearly their subjection to the mayor and his deputies. But either the powers conferred upon the civic authorities were not sufficiently great, or the tailors presumed too much upon their privileges; at any rate the result was a conflict between the two factions which was waged fiercely for some time, until in the twenty-second year of his reign, after repeated appeals from the city authorities, King Edward finally ordered the tailors' charter to be quashed, and the rival parties came to terms.[2]

Nevertheless such instances seem to be the exception in the general course of development. For the most part the power of the municipality was acknowledged without need of royal interference. Even in Exeter the example of the tailors did not arouse the other crafts to like aggressions. Indeed the cordwainers were so completely under the domination of the city officials that their masters and wardens were compelled to apply annually to the newly-elected borough officers for a renewal of their customary rights.[3] In Coventry, the

[1] *Annals of the Barber-Surgeons*, p. 52.

[2] Smith, *op. cit.*, pp. 300–330.

[3] *Ibid.*, pp. 331–334.

dyers, who had been at continual warfare with the municipality during the century, had their by-laws completely annulled.[1] In Southampton the bakers' craft was entirely under the supervision of the town.[2] The Salisbury tailors, though chartered by the crown, had their letters patent confirmed by the local governors, the Bishop of Salisbury and the Dean and Chapter.[3]

This survey of the general situation following the act of 1437 puts us in a position to judge safely the effects of the policy of Henry VI and of his successor, Edward IV, upon the status of the craft gild. We can fairly assert that the former was altogether in favor of municipal regulation and oversight of the gilds, and that therefore no change in their position is perceptible during his reign. Edward IV, to be sure, in a few instances granted almost unlimited powers to important crafts in different parts of the realm, yet in actual practice, as we have seen, those organizations were politic enough for the most part to acknowledge dependence upon civic authority. In cases of conflicting rights, the craft gilds were invariably forced to yield to the municipal power. On the other hand, the study of craft ordinances drawn up after 1437 certainly shows no abating on the part of the gilds of claims to their earlier privileges. The act of Henry VI had evidently laid no new restraints upon them.

Yet what called this legislation of 1437 into existence?

[1] *Eng. Hist. Rev.*, vol. IX, p. 637. So troublesome were these Coventry dyers that the city authorities appealed to Parliament for permission to have the "twenty-four who elected the mayor" choose two drapers and two dyers to overlook the craft and "present them for any fault or confederacy." *Rot. Parl.*, vol. iv, p. 75.

[2] Davies, *Southampton*, p. 264.

[3] *Wiltshire Notes and Queries*, vol. i, p. 30.

Why was the justice of the peace given jurisdiction in craft matters, if it was to be merely a name and not a reality? Were craft gilds perhaps growing up in rural districts, in villages, where the oversight of such an official was required to bring them under competent jurisdiction? There is no evidence to prove this. Were the methods of the London crafts quoted by Professor Cunningham responsible for the act? But even in London, at that period as far as craft ordinances or town records show, city authorities and craft gilds were working together in comparative harmony. Did the measure, as Brentano has suggested, prevent great numbers of villeins then crowding into the towns from ever becoming independent masters?[1] If this were true, it could not be regarded as antagonistic to craft gilds and hence would not be included in a discussion of legislation adverse to that system, since the government would thereby be acting wholly in accord with the desires of the craft masters, and thus of their gilds.

Possibly the presence within many of the boroughs of foreign-born craftsmen who were introducing new gilds may have necessitated legislative action to confirm the municipal control. On the other hand it may well be that the measure was demanded simply by public opinion. The craft-gild system was intent upon the monopoly of trade and industry throughout the realm. For this purpose the gilds had come into being and won privileges from the national as well as from the municipal government. In their dealings, moreover, they had naturally been neither slow nor timid in interpreting in the broadest fashion any powers granted to them. Legislative acts to prohibit their monopolistic practices had already

[1] Smith, *op. cit.*, cxl.

been found necessary.[1] It was but natural that the general public as consumers of gild products should hold those organizations responsible for whatever discomfort or hardship they suffered through the excesses of the gilds. In accordance with this reasoning the measure may be regarded as an effort to check further fresh aggressions of craft gilds.

The purpose of the act must after all remain uncertain. The effect we can better estimate; as we have seen it was practically nil. The provision for the endorsement of craft by-laws introduced no novel method of procedure, so no changes can be expected from its execution. The statute can scarcely be reckoned as a factor in the decay of craft gilds in the fifteenth century. All that can be asserted is that it was probably an attempt in the interest of the general public to hinder monopolistic craft practice, which proved unsuccessful in actual operation. As Professor Cunningham has said, it was a sign that the system of craft gilds was beginning to get out of gearing.[2] Mr. Cunningham's qualification, however, that this was true at any rate in London, puts perhaps too narrow a limit upon conditions which by that time must have been general throughout the realm.

[1] Such enactments as 5 Richard II, i, c. 4, 5; 6 Richard II, i, c. 12. They were, however, repealed in the seventh year of Richard's reign. *Rot. Parl.*, vol. iii, p. 161.

[2] *Growth of Eng. Ind. and Com.*, vol. i, p. 337.

CHAPTER II

THE POLICY OF THE EARLY TUDORS TOWARD CRAFT GILDS

The advent of the Tudors to the English throne brought no immediate change in the relations established between the government and craft gilds. Not until the closing years of Henry VII's reign, when the sixteenth century was well begun, did the Tudor policy, which aimed at bringing all social forces directly under national control, make itself felt in relation to the gild system. Up to that time craft organizations had continued their progress in the path mapped out for them in the previous century. All the forces of the age tended, seemingly, to strengthen borough or local control over industrial interests. The mayor and aldermen still retained the right of overseeing and recording craft by-laws, as we find them doing in London for the carpenters,[1] the coopers,[2] and the tailors, who are now designated by the high-sounding title of "The Master and Wardens of Merchant Taylors." Indeed the large grant of power and privileges bestowed upon the last-named association in 1502, enjoins the company to do nothing that might prejudice the authority of the mayor of the city.[3] In other boroughs, such as Kingston-upon-Hull,[4] where craft organizations appear on record for the first time in

[1] Jupp and Pocock, *The Worshipful Company of Carpenters*, p. 344.

[2] Firth, *Coopers Company of London*, p. 12.

[3] Clode, *Memorials of Merchant Taylors*, p. 197.

[4] Lambert, *Two Thousand Years of Gild Life*, pp. 204-7, 215-17.

1490, compositions made by those bodies with the city authorities show the seal of the "mairaltie." In Exeter,[1] at that same time, the barber-surgeons and the weavers were being incorporated by the town officials, and four years later the haberdashers obtained the same favor.

Legislation reflects also the feeling of the time, in its insistence upon the approval of craft by-laws by municipal authority. An act of Henry VII, in granting powers of search to the Norwich worsted shearers, commanded that they make no ordinances which the mayor and his officers might consider either unnecessary or unprofitable.[2]

1. *Intervention of the Government under Henry VII. Act of 1503–4.*—With the year 1503–4 King Henry inaugurated a change in his industrial policy. Realizing, perhaps, the inadequacy of the restraint previously exercised over the conduct of the craft gilds, the government again intervened by means of a legislative act, which indicated a new policy directed toward a more perfect regulation of craft gilds in their relation to the public.[3] The preamble asserts that the act was necessary, because, since the expiration of the statute of Henry VI,[4] craft gilds had

[1] *Western Antiquary*, vol. iv, p. 188.

[2] 11 Henry VII, c. 11.

[3] 19 Henry VII, c. 7. This act recited the complaint of the former statute, of Henry VI, that "masters, wardens and people of gilds, fraternities, and other companies corporate, dwelling in divers parts of the realm, often times by colour of rule and governance to them granted and confirmed by charters and letters patent of divers kings, make among themselves many unlawful and unreasonable ordinances as well *in prices of wares* as other things, for their own singular profit and to the common hurt and damage of the people . . ." Not only is the complaint of the earlier act repeated here, but the direct charge of unlawfulness in the *prices of wares* is made.

[4] This statement leads us to suppose that the framers of the statute of Henry VII considered that that of Henry VI had expired. As we have seen, the earlier act had been passed to endure as long as it should please

continued to make unlawful ordinances "in prices" as well as in other matters, which, while redounding to the benefit of the gilds, acted to the "common hurt." For the remedy of these abuses the statute prescribed that thereafter gild by-laws should be examined, approved and registered by the Chancellor, the Treasurer and Chief Justices of either Bench, or three of them, or by the Justices of Assize in their circuit. Nor was this the only check upon the craft gilds. The act further provided that "none of the same bodies corporate take upon them to make any acts or ordinances to restrain any person or persons to sue to the King's Highness, or to any of his Courts, for due remedy to be had in their causes, nor put nor execute any penalty or punishment upon any of them for any such suit to be made," under penalty.

By the enactment, therefore, not only were the highest executive officials in the land set in authority over craft by-laws, but the king's judicial officials were thenceforth to have direct jurisdiction in cases of craft dispute.

the king. Whether this clause placed any time limit upon the execution of the provisions of the Henry VI act, we do not know. The only legislation under Edward IV, so far as we have observed, which had any bearing upon the subject of craft gilds, is the act of his first Parliament, 1 Edward IV, c. 1, confirming the validity of certain laws of his predecessors, namely, "that all manner of liberties, privileges . . . not revoked or repealed nor adnulled by authority of Parliament or otherwise by process of law granted in the times of Henry IV, V, or VI, . . . to any Mayor, Bailiff . . . commonalty and citizens . . . and to the Masters, Brethren and Sisters of Guilds and Fraternities, Masters and Commonalty, their Heirs and Successors, and Wardens and Masters of Crafts . . . and to the Successors of every of them, having corporation, by whatsoever name or names they or any of them be called or named in any of the said Grants, they shall be in like Strength and Virtue, as if they had been granted by any King or Kings lawfully reigning in this Realm." It would seem as if this act were sufficient to keep the statute of Henry VI in force, so far as it ever had been observed.

Local authority was no longer deemed sufficient to prevent craft aggression. The principal magistrates of the king must, in the future, lend the weight of their sanction to craft by-laws, before they were put into operation, and the judgment of the royal tribunals was needed to convict one finally of craft offences.

What occasioned this change of policy at this time, and what was its effect upon the gild system? Here again theories have not been lacking to account for the act. The definite charge enunciated in it, that the gilds had been guilty of unlawfulness in the "prices of things," has suggested an interpretation, of which writers have not been slow to avail themselves.

Busch, for example, attempts to show that the statute was due to a selfish action on the part of the London bakers, which had caused a rise in the price of bread not to be attributed to any scarcity of wheat or corn. Just what these bakers may have done does not appear. Busch argues, however, that the statute of Henry VI had expired, and that this deed of the bakers possibly recalled to men's minds the earlier law; hence followed its re-enactment.[1]

A curious contrast to this view, and an interesting contemporary conception of the antecedents of the act of Henry VII, is found in the prosy narrative of the Recorder of the London Merchant Taylors.[2] He explains at great length and with much care how, while craft members adhered to their old practice of not taking suits into the king's courts, but allowing the governors of their crafts to settle matters in dispute, "good obedience and perfect love and charity" had held sway among craft brethren. But into this state of peace and brotherly love

[1] *England under the Tudors*, p. 257. [2] Clode, *op. cit.*, p. 199.

the Recorder of London and one of the knights of Parliament craftily penetrated. Inasmuch as this practice had prejudiced the interests of the "learned men" of the city, the Recorder and the knight had procured the insertion of the last provision in the statute, in order that the "learned men" (presumably the lawyers) might no longer be deprived of the emolument which would fall to them if suits arising out of trade disagreements were brought to them for settlement.

In obedience to the statute prompted by the greatness of the interests at stake, the Merchant Taylors had this same Recorder compile a "book" of their by-laws. In 1507 this obtained the proper legal endorsement. Some of their fellow crafts in London also complied, the mercers [1] almost immediately after the passage of the act. The salters,[2] the vintners,[3] and the coopers[4] delayed to secure approval for their by-laws until 1507.

Outside of London, as far as there is any evidence, proper endorsement of craft laws seems to have been procured from the justices of assize in their circuits. The records of such endorsement, however, are of a much later date. In some cases the approval of the civic authorities had evidently been sought first. The Oxford butchers in 1536 petitioned "Ye Judges of the Assize" to oversee and examine the orders made by the master and wardens of their gild, and approved by the mayor and three aldermen.[5] Indeed, it is sometimes stated that the town seal should be put to craft by-laws in order that the justices of assize might allow them. The

[1] Hazlitt, *The Great Livery Companies*, p. 180. [2] *Ibid.*, p. 294.

[3] *London and Middlesex Archæological Society*, vol. iii, p. 438.

[4] Firth, *Coopers Company*, p. 110. Later, in 1581, this company's by-laws again show such confirmation; as do the vintners' in 1594.

[5] Turner, *Records of Oxford*, p. 144.

Oxford glovers record such a proceeding.[1] On a Shrewsbury document the signatures of the town bailiffs, approving the ordinances of the mercers, are followed immediately by those of the justices.[2] The signatures of the same officers were obtained by the Ludlow stitchmen, when in 1569 their "composission" was renewed in accordance with the provisions of the statute.[3] On the other hand, the Gloucester tanners seem to have compromised in 1543 by inserting among their by-laws the article, that if any of those should prove to be opposed to the king's law, or the common weal of the town, the justices of assize might alter them.[4]

In many boroughs, Kingston-upon-Hull, Bristol and Exeter, for instance, no endorsement of craft by-laws by any of these central officials is to be discovered. There, as in other towns where isolated records furnish testimony, craft gilds followed the old fifteenth century policy, and secured approval from their local governors only. Such was the conduct of the cutlers of Hallomshire, who obtained the assent of their "Lorde," the Earl of Shrewsbury, to ordinances prepared about 1590.[5]

[1] In 1562 it was "enacted . . . by the hole body of the Counsaill that the Towne seale shalbe put to the boke of the Mystery of glovers which was reade in this howse so that the same boke be allowed by the justyces of the Assises." *Ibid.*, p. 288.

[2] *Shropshire Archæological Society Transactions*, vol. v, pp. 284-5.

[3] *Journal British Archæological Association*, vol. xxiv, p. 328.

[4] *Transactions Bristol and Gloucester Archæological Society*, vol. xiii, p. 266.

[5] "Ordinances made and agreed uppon the first daye of Sept., 32 Eliz., as well by all the hole fellowshippe and Co. of Cutlers as alsoe by th' assente of the righte honorable George, Erle of Shrewsburye, Lorde and Owner of the said Lordshippe of Hallomshire, for the better relief and comodytie of the poorer sorte of the saide fellowshippe." Hunter's *Hallomshire*, p. 150.

In many cases proper endorsement, when it came, was a matter of much later date.[1]

The preponderance of evidence thus goes to show that the act providing for endorsement of craft regulations by the king's officials was by no means rigidly enforced. Moreover, as we shall see later, even where it was obeyed, no change resulted in the character of those regulations. Nor is there any record of the disapproval of craft ordinances by the high authorities. Consequently in cases where proper approval was obtained,[2] as truly as where it was not,[3] craft codes consisted merely of laws of an earlier date, with certain new rules appended, which, if anything, were increasingly beneficial to craft authorities.

In view of these facts, what influence can be ascribed to government action so far in forwarding the decay of craft gilds? The very necessity for this second act was a sign of the efficacy of the methods pursued by the gilds up to that time. Their continued encroachment forced the government again to interfere in an effort to hold

[1] As is evident from the records of the joiners and carpenters of Worcester. Smith, *English Gilds*, p. 210. Professor Ashley thinks that the fact that later annals of the gilds show proper approval, proves sufficiently that all new gild statutes were submitted for the approval of the chief executive authorities at London. But this seems a rather summary dismissal of the question. *Eng. Econ. Hist.*, vol. ii, p. 160.

[2] Compare the ordinances of the Merchant Taylors of London, 1507 and 1613. Clode, *Memorials*, pp. 201-226.

[3] The compositions of the weavers of Kingston-upon-Hull are on record for 1490 and 1564. The earlier articles in the composition of 1564 are almost identical with those of 1490, the only apparent difference being an increase in the amount of the fines prescribed in the later document. For example, in 1490, any weaver at "his upsett," *i. e.*, opening a separate shop, must pay iiis., iiiid. But, by 1564, the charge for the same privilege has risen to vis., viiid., to be paid to the town's chamber and vis., viiid. to the occupation. The fine in 1564, therefore, is just four times the earlier amount. Lambert, *op. cit.*, p. 205.

them in check. The need of this re-enactment, in a more stringent form, of the provisions of Henry VI, makes it evident that the gilds had amended not a whit their former aggressive attitude, notwithstanding the obligation of obtaining municipal approval for their by-laws. It is interesting to note that whereas the nature of the unlawful and unreasonable ordinances attributed to the gilds in the fifteenth century had been left vague by this statute of the early sixteenth century, a distinct grievance finds voice in the complaint that unlawfulness was practiced in the prices charged for wares. The framers of the later statute, while rehearsing in their preamble the act of Henry VI, inserted in it this specific charge of unlawful prices, words not really to be seen in the earlier act, as found upon the statute book.[1] Since, therefore, this clause appears only in the second enactment, it is natural to infer that at the beginning of the sixteenth century the question of price had become a peculiar source of discontent. Upon the craft gilds, vitally concerned with all market transactions, the blame for an unsatisfactory state of affairs inevitably fell. Was the accusation just? Did craft gilds fix the price at which commodities were to be sold? If not, what agency at this stage of English industrial life had the determination of prices for ordinary wares?

This question has naturally occupied the attention of

[1] Professor Cunningham is, therefore, mistaken when he attributes this charge of unlawful prices to the statute of Henry VI. Miss Ellen A. McArthur also reads into the Henry VI act the charge of unreasonable ordinances in prices. To quote her words "crafts as early as 1436 lost independent control over prices for a time." Moreover, she interprets the unlawful ordinances of the Henry VII act to be in *prices of wages*, but the charge makes no mention of wages. It distinctly says *prices of wares* [weyres]. "Prices at Woodstock in 1604." Note 2. *English Historical Review*, vol. xiii, p. 711.

previous writers upon craft gilds. Professor Ashley, in his consideration of it, acknowledges the difficulty of any attempt to ascertain the exact extent to which gilds may be accused of having exercised such a power, with or without authorization. But he concludes that no matter to what extent they may ever have exercised it, by this act of Henry VII they were completely deprived of it.[1] Yet the question can by no means be so summarily dismissed, if we are to estimate accurately the effect of such legislation upon the system which the gilds had established.

A conscientious search of all available records has failed to reveal a single instance where the crafts claimed the right to determine the price of a commodity upon gild authority alone. This is no truer after the passage of this act of 1503–4 than before. In the rare instances where mention is made of the price to be charged for an article, reference is in some way distinctly made to the power of the civic authority.[2] Since craft gilds, therefore, as far as one may gather from their ordinances, do not appear to have much concerned themselves with the question of price, upon whom did the decision of such subjects rest, and where may one find the record?

Never, perhaps, is the static condition of early mediæval life so clearly illustrated as when in a search for the earliest signs of the existence of such a power one meets the baffling statement that prices are to be reasonable. Desire for knowledge as to the mediæval standard of rea-

[1] *Eng. Econ. Hist.*, vol. ii, p. 160.

[2] For example, in the ordinances of the "Berbruers" of Kingston-upon-Hull in the time of Mary, it is ordained that "it shalbe laufull to the Mayor and aldermen, justices at all tymes to sett the price of doble bere and merchants bere, oyerwise called shippe bere." Lambert, *op. cit.*, p. 226.

sonableness in price is rewarded by the order that in case of doubt inquiry is to be made concerning the price in use in some adjacent district. In short, we are brought up against the fact that to the mediæval man prices were a matter of custom. In other words, local tradition was largely responsible for the price charged for a commodity.

With the establishment of the Norman régime, the promulgation of the assizes of bread, wine, ale and other articles of food, gave local authorities control over the prices for those commodities. One of the privileges contained in many of the charters granted to English boroughs was that of enforcing these assizes. The control of the question of price seems to be a royal prerogative.[1] This theory is further confirmed by the record upon the Exchequer rolls of Henry III of the payment of a fine by the vintners of Hereford,[2] in order that wine might be sold for a stated sum in that locality. On the other hand, during this same century, the gild merchant of Leicester forbade the fullers to make any "fixed assize" for the price at which a yard of cloth might be sold, showing that with the grant of a gild merchant the burgesses assumed the right of prescribing at least the price at which a commodity might not be sold.[3] Even if they did not possess the right to determine price, they assumed a power of general supervision.

[1] The charter granted Bristol in 1373 emphasizes the power of the municipality in the "assize or assay of wines, bread or ale, or any other victuals, infringed in the said town, or suburbs, or for default of yards, balances, weights, or measures whatsoever . . ." *Little Red Book*, vol. ii, p. 122.

[2] The Vintners of Hereford fined in XL s. to have the King's grant that a Sextericum of Wine might be sold for X d. in Hereford for the space of a Year. Madox. *Hist. of Exchequer*, vol. 1, p. 418.

[3] Bateson, *Records of Leicester*, vol. i, p. 89.

When the subject of price really became serious the national government expressed its sentiments in statutory ruling. A growing gravity in the situation was first apparent immediately after the Black Death, when the forces making for change, which had doubtless been quietly gathering strength for centuries, suddenly came into prominence, and the question of the price of labor and food, the two fundamental concerns of human life, demanded careful consideration. Even at this time, however, the government was anxious to keep conditions as they had been before the advent of disturbing times. By the new statute, prices were still to be reasonable and customary.[1] The earliest legislation on the subject applied simply to the trades which dealt with articles of food, and in keeping with the usual methods of more ancient laws and town charters, gave mayors and bailiffs power to punish offenders.

Eight years later conditions in London called for special regulation of the same question, and the national government here again gave the civic authorities jurisdiction for enforcing the statute.[2] At this time, in 1350, not only did city authorities actually determine the price to be charged for food, but they also issued an ordinance setting the price of various articles of wearing apparel, of shoes, boots, spurs and gloves of different qualities.[3] In Bristol a fourteenth century Town Proclamation, containing many regulations for the trade and general

[1] 23 Edward III, c. 6. "Butchers, fishmongers, hostelers, brewers, bakers, pulters and all other sellers of victual shall be bound to sell the same victual for a reasonable price, having respect to the price that such victual be sold at in the places adjoining . . . mayors and bailiffs of cities, boroughs . . . shall have power to inquire of all and singular which shall in anything offend the same."

[2] 31 Edward III, St. 1, c. 10.

[3] Riley, *Memorials of London*, p. 256.

welfare of the city's interests, fixed the price to be charged for different articles of food.[1] In Kingston-upon-Hull,[2] among "the most antient laws, ordinances and constitutions," proclaimed every year in the market place, were articles defining the prices to be paid for candles and for ale. Among the "Old Usages of Winchester" we find a statement of the price at which coarse cloth was to be sold, with variations for the different seasons of the year.[3]

In the fifteenth century craft-gild records show that municipal authorities exercised this power even within the sphere of gild interests. The London vintners were ordered to make known a maximum price at which they would sell their commodities.[4] The brewers, in 1422, were summoned before the mayor in the Guildhall on a charge of excessive prices exacted for their ale.[5] In York, early in the century, the bakers had to take instructions as to the price of bread from the mayor.[6] Toward the end of the century statutes are no longer concerned with the price of articles of food alone. At

[1] *Little Red Book*, vol. ii, p. 224. Bakers are to sell two loaves of bread for 1 d; brewers to make good ale and keep the Assize; they shall sell a gallon of the best ale in a barrel for 1½ d. Cooks shall sell a goose well roasted for 4 d.

[2] No one was to presume to sell a pound of candles for more than one penny or a gallon of the best ale for more than the same. Lambert, *op. cit.*, p. 222.

[3] Smith, *op. cit.*, p. 350.

[4] In 1416 the four masters of the company were enjoined to assemble their citizens and make known to them that "they shall not sell white or red wine at a dearer price than 8 pence per gallon, or any sweet wines dearer than 12 pence, on pain of forfeiture of their vessels and imprisonment." *Trans. London and Middlesex Arch. Soc.*, vol. iii, p. 417.

[5] Herbert, *Twelve Great Livery Cos.*, vol. i, p. 56.

[6] *Archæological Review*, vol. i, p. 124.

that period the excessive prices demanded by drapers and tailors throughout the realm brought out an act[1] proclaiming a maximum sum for such wares. The hat and cap makers were also subjected to similar legislation.

Throughout the sixteenth century, statutes for the regulation of the methods of manufacture provided likewise penalties for unusual prices.[2] Special statutes still governed the prices to be charged for articles of food and drink.[3] Toward the middle of the century, mercantile enterprises by the municipalities were encouraged and authorized by acts of Parliament. In this way the mayor and citizens of Norwich were incorporated a fellowship for the manufacture of cloth.[4] In York, in the time of Elizabeth, the civic authorities began a spinning and weaving business, and ere long complaints were heard of the high prices they demanded for their cloth.[5] Town records throughout the century show the municipality frequently concerning itself with the promulgation of proper prices. In 1507 the Southampton chandlers were to supply the town with candles at a stated price.

[1] 4 Henry VII, c. 8. Because those crafts "sellen a yerde of cloth at excessive price . . . to the grete hurte it is ordeyned . . . that noo persone selle within this Reame at retaille a brode yerde of wollen clothe . . . above the price of XVI s." By c. 9, "not above XX pens" is to be charged for the "best hatte."

[2] Such was 34 and 35 Henry VIII, c. 6, an "Acte for the True Making of Pynnes."

[3] 24 Henry VIII, c. 3, providing for the sale of "Fleche," gave authority to the Lord Chancellor, Justices of Assize, of the Peace, Mayors, Bailiffs, *etc.*, to lower prices.

[4] By act of 1 and 2 Philip and Mary, c. 14, for the making of "Russelles Sattens" and "Fustian of Naples," the fellowship was "to punish offenders according to rules and ordinances which shall from time to time be made within the city by the mayor, the wardens and the fellowship necessary for the true making of the same."

[5] *Eng. Hist. Rev.*, vol. xii, p. 440.

In 1518 the contract was revised.[1] In 1552 the Oxford chandlers had the price of their commodity fixed by the city.[2] In Liverpool, in 1584, the price of ale was fixed by municipal ordinance,[3] and two years later it again received attention.[4]

It would seem, therefore, that as far as the crown by proclamation, and Parliament by statute, and the municipality by ordinance, could establish a fixed price for the sale of commodities, the three powers had co-operated to do so. At all events, whenever the question of price is mentioned in any commercial connection throughout these centuries, it is either in statute books or in series of town ordinances. As we have seen, the prices for articles of food had been from early times a matter for government and municipal ruling. Later, with the rise of manufactures, the government supervised both the process of manufacture and the price set upon the finished product. Its action was not always systematic or continuous, but it was sufficient to establish the principle of its right to act. Moreover, as has already been said, not one craft ordinance, either before or after the act of Henry VII, is to be found claiming the power to determine the price of an article on gild authority alone. As far as records demonstrate, therefore, there seems to be no reason for asserting with Professor Ashley that the power of determining prices was from the time of the act lost by craft gilds. No statute indicates that they had ever possessed such power. However much in their

[1] Davies, *Southampton*, p. 270.

[2] The "Justiciar" ordained that butchers sell tallow for xvi d. a stone, under penalty, and that chandlers sell candles at 2 d. a pound. Turner, *Records of Oxford*, p. 212.

[3] Picton, *Liverpool Records*, p. 61.

[4] *Ibid.*, p. 87.

private market dealings they may have transgressed the laws fixing price, their ordinances record no official resistance.

Perhaps the final test of the effectiveness of the provision that endorsement of craft by-laws should be obtained from the chief magistrates of the land is to be sought in an investigation of the fate of that other provision in which, as we have seen, contemporaries were especially interested, namely, that craft members were not to be restrained from bringing their suits into the king's courts. On this subject we have direct evidence furnished by craft ordinances. The ironmongers of London, in accordance with the requirement, had their by-laws duly approved and endorsed by the Lord Chancellor, the Lord Chief Justice, and the Chief Justices of the Common Pleas. These laws, however, were the same as those recorded in 1498, with some additions, and contained the following provision:

None of the said Companie shall sue, molest or trouble anie other of the misterie, for any private thing, matter or cause . . without license of wardens of the same company for the time being . . first had and obtained, upon payne to lose and paye . . twentie shillings . . Also . . if any of the said fellowshipp owe money to any other of the same fellowshipp, or commit toward him or them any trespass or offence, that then they and every one of them . . grieved or hurt shall complayne to the wardens of the lyverye of the said company . . and then it is ordeyned that they within convenient tyme shall either compound and fynish the matter between them or else geve the plaintiff license to sue elsewhere as to himself and his learned counsell shall be thought most mete.[1]

[1] Nichols, *The Worshipful Company of Ironmongers*, pp. 125, 131.

These articles certainly did not conform to the letter of the new law, to make no mention of its spirit. Nor can an appreciable difference be seen between them and the rule in force a century earlier among the barber-surgeons of the same city.[1] There in case of differences between craft members, no "pursuit at the common law" was to be begun until the aggrieved party should make his complaint to the master and wardens of the gilds; then if the matter were not "finished within six days," it was to be lawful for either party to "take the benefice of the common law" within the city.

The by-laws of the Shrewsbury mercers, fully endorsed and approved in 1515, were simply a repetition of those drawn up in the time of Edward IV. Among them was a provision for the trial of dissensions among craft brethren in preference to going before the bailiffs of the town.[2] In Coventry,[3] in 1518, the mysteries were compelled to make the mayor arbiter in disputes between offenders against craft law and the gild wardens. Here the municipality assumed the same direction over craft matters which it had taken in 1457, when, because of troubles resulting from the special craft courts, the Leet had declared that thereafter masters should bring no suit in any special court against one of their craftsmen until the mayor should have heard the matter and "licensed the suit to be had." As late as 1564 one of the craft ordinances for

[1] *Annals of Barber-Surgeons*, p. 45.

[2] The bailiffs of the borough viewed and examined the ordinances and "perceiving that the same appears to be good, laudable . . . as far as in them lies," granted them to the wardens, searchers and other officers of the craft. After their signatures appear those of the "Kyng's Justices of Hys Comen Plays," who also approve, allow, and confirm them. *Shrop. Arch. Soc. Trans.*, vol. viii, pp. 284–5.

[3] Harris, *Life in an Old Eng. Town*, p. 263.

the weavers of Kingston-upon-Hull forbids suit being brought in "none other courte owte of this towne."[1]

This act of Henry VII cannot, therefore, be considered as really influential in preventing craft gilds from claiming and exercising jurisdiction over their members, even when the high authority nominated in the act was given full chance to see to its enforcement. For, although some of the important crafts did comply, so far as to have their constitutions properly approved and registered, the proceeding seems to have been largely a matter of form and perhaps of payment.[2] The companies apparently had not the least trouble in securing the official seal, and made no effort to bring their regulations within the letter of the law. But in the majority of cases craft ordinances probably never came before the national officials, and continued under the supervision of borough authorities.[3] In some few places, like Shrews-

[1] Lambert, *op. cit.*, p. 207.

[2] The Merchant Taylors of London, in 1612, employed an effective method of propitiating the powers that be. Upon the advice of their Recorder, in order to obtain the Chancellor's approval of their "booke of Ordinance," the gild authorities decreed that that dignitary be "presented with some remembrance from the Company for the better furtherance and fynishinge of that busyness." The form which the "remembrance" took was the gift of "tenne double sufferants in gould." The gild also voted that "what other monies shalbe disbursed by the consent of the Master and Wardens to any Judge or Counsellor for the said business shall be paide by our Master." Clode, *op. cit.*, p. 546.

[3] Writers have questioned whether the crafts ever obeyed the ruling of the acts of either Henry VI or Henry VII. Lambert, for instance, speaking for the gilds of Kingston-upon-Hull, whose ordinances from 1490–1723 are extant, finds no authorization by any but the mayor of the town. He, however, classes the acts together, and draws no distinction between the officials entrusted with the endorsement of craft by-laws by the two acts. *Two Thousand Years*, p. 188. The sixteenth century record of the weavers' craft of Newcastle-upon-Tyne shows that, in 1527, their ordinances obtained confirmation "by the authority

bury and Oxford, they received both municipal and national authorization, the latter from the justices in their circuits. If any one of these officials ever objected to any craft ordinance, his protest has at least left no trace upon available records.

Although no important modification of the practices in vogue among craft gilds can thus be ascribed to the act of 1503–4, does the fact of its enactment prove any hostility of motive on the part of the government? Is the spirit that manifested itself in the previous century, when Henry VI's parliament interfered to stop craft aggression, at work again now? The crafts had continued their former methods of aggrandizement, growing perhaps more reckless in their career of license which local authorities were proving totally unable to check. Public opinion again made its grievances heard, this time in a more definite complaint. The government again felt called upon to intervene, and to provide a remedy. In keeping with its whole general policy, it attempted to bring craft organizations more closely under national control, and to this end brought its highest executive officers into play.

This action, however, was but a part of the whole industrial policy of the English government. Certain rules for the supervision of trade and industry developing out of custom and experience were gradually becom-

of the Mayor, Sheriff and Aldermen, Justices of the Peace, with the consent of their own Body." This is the only mention thus far found of the justice of the peace as one of the authorities engaged in authorizing craft by-laws. In this case, however, it is the city officials, the mayor, sheriff and aldermen, who act as justices of the peace. Moreover, at the time of this record, the act of Henry VII had called for endorsement by national executive officers, so that the Newcastle authorities were not carrying out the letter of the law. Walford, *Gilds*, p. 199.

ing clearly defined in statutory enactments, to which the commercial classes of England were expected to pay obedience. The gilds, as bodies of men directly engaged in mercantile pursuits, were not to be treated as exceptions. When universal complaint testified to their persistent infringement of the laws, the government again attempted to check their continuous aggressions. In so doing it followed the lines pursued in the previous century. But to attribute any real hostility on the part of the English government toward the gild system as such indicates a failure to appreciate its entire industrial policy.

2. *Intervention by the Government under Henry VIII.*

1. *Act of 1531.*—The foregoing interpretation of the character of the action of the government and its effects upon craft gilds is confirmed by conditions a quarter of a century later. In 1531 craft abuses again called for governmental interference. The statute enacted in this year complained that, since the time of the legislation of Henry VII,[1] the fellowships had continued to make ordinances "after their owne senester myndes and pleasure, contrarie the menyng of the acte aforesayd and to the greate hurte of the Kynges true subjectes." The particular cause for complaint at this time, however, lay in the internal conduct of gild affairs. Those organizations had been charging their apprentices, upon the

[1] 22 Henry VIII, c. 4. "Wardens and fellowships have made acts and ordinances that every prentise shall pay at his first entry in their common hall to the wardens of the same fellowship, some of them XL shillings, some XXX s., some XX s., some XIII s. IV d. . . . therefore, hereafter no master, wardens, or fellowships of crafts . . . are to take henceforth of any prentise . . . or persons for the entry of any prentise, above the sum of 2 s. 6 d. nor of his entry when his years term is expired and ended above 3 s. 4 d. . . . "

expiration of their terms of service, almost prohibitive fees for membership in the gilds, thus preventing many from enjoying the privilege of entrance.

Although this phase of gild misbehavior was now for the first time publicly recognized by the government, it had been an object of solicitude in the gilds themselves as early as 1480. At that time the Shrewsbury mercers themselves had attempted to deal with the evil, because they considered the fines assessed upon their apprentices "at their entries to be maysters" to be exorbitant. Protest was registered in their by-laws against these charges, which were thereafter to be "dymynished and refowrmed."[1] Municipal authority also had at various times concerned itself with this abuse. The Coventry Leet had tried to overcome the exclusive tendencies evident in the borough by fixing the sum chargeable upon apprentices at six shillings and eight pence.[2] Oxford,[3] in 1531, the year of the government act, had determined "by the more part of the Counsell of the Towne" that no greater fee than twenty shillings should be taken for admittance into craft membership within that city or suburbs, upon penalty of paying to the town's coffer double the sum of the amount charged.

2. *Act of 1537.*—Another effort was made by the government six years after the last statute, to deal with substantially the same evil, though now it had taken on a

[1] *Shrop. Arch. Soc. Trans.*, vol. viii, p. 284.

[2] Harris, *op. cit.*, p. 273.

[3] Turner, *Records*, p. 107. "Noc occupation for crafts within the Towne of Oxford and the suburbys of the same shall take of any person that shall come to be brother of theyr crafts above the sum of XX s., and yf the same crafts or occupacion take any more than the same XX s. that then the same occupacion or crafte to forfeyte to the usse of the Towne XL s."

slightly different form. The act of 1537,[1] after a rehearsal of the two previous statutes and their evasions by craft gilds, charged craft masters "with practise to defraud," because they required apprentices at the conclusion of their term of service to swear not to set up separate establishments without a license from the master and wardens of their craft. This custom was forbidden under penalty.

The need of such legislation by the government of Henry VIII seems but added evidence of the futility of national intervention along the lines adopted by his predecessors. Prohibitions had by the acts of Henry VI and Henry VII been directed against the practice of making unlawful ordinances. Yet the gilds had continued to make them, and had added to their number some that were recognized as direct invasions of the rights of their own workmen. This practice, moreover, had been going on in the face of municipal and national inspection of craft by-laws. In Oxford the evil had been so serious that it had evoked municipal attention, as we have seen, at about the time that the national legislature was attempting to deal with the problem. At this point another consideration arises, complicating an effort to estimate accurately the effects of the national intervention.

As we have seen, at Oxford the restriction by craft

[1] 28 Henry VIII, c. 5. The text reads that the fraudulent practices of the gilds caused "prentises after their years expiration to swear that they shall not set up or open any shop house, nor occupie as freemen without assente and lycence of the Master and Wardens, upon payne of forfeiting their freedom or other like penalty, causing more expense than they were originally put to, in obtaining their freedom, to their great hurt." . . . For remedy it was provided that "no Wardens nor rulers compel or cause any prentise to make oath or otherwise, that he will not set up or keep shop nor occupie as a freeman, without license of the Master, Wardens, nor take any fees for such freedom upon payne to forfeit for every time that they shall offend. . . ."

masters of the ordinary rights of apprentices by charging fines so exorbitant that they practically prohibited membership in the gilds, attracted the attention of the town authorities, and they straightway provided rules to remedy the evil. Parliament did the same, treating the evil as a national concern. Whereas the nature of the two remedies proposed was the same—punishment by fine—yet the amount of the fine to be levied differed in the national and municipal regulations. At Oxford the sum named was twenty shillings. The government fixed as a maximum penalty three shillings and four pence. Which ruling in such duplication of legislation obtained precedence, especially when the question involved shillings and pence? Since the municipal penalty, however, was more nearly commensurate with the amount of the offence (according to the accusation in the first act of Henry VIII, the charges of the craft gild had reached to forty shillings), we may imagine that if either rule ever became binding upon the gilds, the municipality's, rather than the government's, would prevail. The former power was nearest at hand, and perhaps more capable of enforcing its commands. But after all, perplexities such as these seem not to have troubled the officials charged with the endorsement of craft by-laws. In 1536 the Oxford butchers had their ordinances approved by both municipal officers and the justices in their circuit. Presumption in cases of doubt was probably in favor of deference to municipal rather than to national authority. So much we may conjecture from what we have already seen of English industrial conditions.

The two acts of Henry VIII clearly indicate that craft gilds were in some disgrace, not only for monopolistic practices in market transactions, but also for avarice in the conduct of their internal affairs. Here too the government endeavored to check abuse of gild powers. But the character of the enactment is but one consideration in estimating legislative influence. The degree to which the legislation was enforced presents a far more important phase of the question. Whether these provisions actually played a part in craft life, or figured as nothing but empty regulations upon the English statute-book, cannot with certainty be determined, though a preponderance of such evidence as we have inclines one to the latter supposition. The gilds had been too long in the full enjoyment of their powers and were too vitally connected with both national and municipal interests to allow us to count overmuch upon the influence of any legal enactment. Their entire method of procedure was a triumphant expression of the capabilities inherent in the system. The gild system had prospered for centuries on rights, privileges and licenses from government and municipality, which it had been always free to interpret in the broadest terms.

That, moreover, we are to see nothing in these statutes beyond a desire to check craft encroachments and abuse of powers, is thoroughly clear from the continuance of the government policy of employing craft organizations as agents to enforce the regulations passed from time to time regarding processes of manufacture. As the parties most interested in the development of new industries, craft gilds were given special powers to further the execution of state measures upon such matters. This had been government policy as early at least as Henry VI,[1] and became more conspicuously so when government encouragement during the reign of Edward IV did much to increase home manufactures. The act of 1463, which prohibited importation of ready-made arti-

[1] 2 Henry VI, c. 17, regulating the London goldsmiths' craft, insisted that the mark of every goldsmith be known to his wardens.

cles into the kingdom authorized the masters and wardens of every craft or mystery to keep out of their respective crafts wares made by alien artificers.[1] Special legislation gave craft authorities powers of search to prevent deceptive practices among their craftsmen. The horners of London,[2] for example, and the weavers of Norwich[3] were empowered to search for defective wares, and many other instances might be cited.

Under Henry VIII deceptive practices in manufacture had become so common that complaints of "the impoverishment of the commons" seemed the order of the day. Countless acts continued to confer upon craft officials the same powers of search for goods illegally made.[4] The number of these enactments invoking the aid of the crafts to enforce governmental regulation is but added evidence of the policy of the English government to keep the gild system in full operation and control of industrial undertakings. That, however, the government realized the evil tendencies of the system is apparent from the very existence of the statutes we have just been considering. The gilds were the manufacturing agencies, and their deceptive practices were held responsible for poorly-made goods. Yet while the state's efforts were directed toward providing a cure for the wrong, it still made use of gild officials to carry out its aims. At the same time, it also endeavored to check the abuses complained of within the gilds themselves. In all these efforts, however, the government was concerned merely

[1] 3 Edward IV, c. 4. [2] 4 Edward IV, c. 8. [3] 7 Edward IV.

[4] 3 Henry VIII, c. 10, gave the London curriers right of search for deceptive practices found in their craft, but the measure needed reenactment twenty years later, 24 Henry VIII, c. 1. 24 Henry VIII, gave the wardens of the dyers in every borough in the country right to search out defective goods. 34 Henry VIII, c. 10, granted like powers to York coverlet-makers.

with putting an end to misconduct in the industrial world. Its intervention, therefore, in craft-gild affairs, and its attempt to bring those bodies more directly under national control, was wholly in line with its entire industrial policy. The conduct of the gilds, vitally responsible for many of the evils denounced by the public, came in for its share of restriction. Governmental action, however, can by no means be attributed to any general spirit of hostility toward the gild system or to any desire for its wholesale repression.

CHAPTER III

LATER TUDOR POLICY AS A FACTOR IN THE DECAY OF CRAFT GILDS

After the reign of Henry VIII no effort was made to put a check upon craft gilds by a re-enactment of any of the statutes discussed in the previous chapters. This may have been a tacit acknowledgment of the fruitlessness of former attempts, or perhaps it was a part of a deliberate policy to show the fraternities greater favor. At any rate, we hear no more of the need of any similar restraint upon craft aggression.

1. *Action of the Government of Edward VI. Act of 1547.*—In the meantime the Reformation had struck its blow at the gild system. At one time this was considered to have been fatal to the craft as well as to other gilds, but that opinion no longer obtains. The act of 1547 expressly exempted craft gilds from its operation, confiscating only such portions of their possessions as had been devoted to religious purposes.[1] However great a deprivation this may have meant,[2] the

[1] Professor Cunningham believed that the act of Edward VI (1 Ed. VI, c. 14) gave English craft gilds their death-blow. *Growth of Eng. Ind.*, vol. i, pp. 464-5. In the latest edition of his volume on *Modern Times*, Mr. Cunningham still considers it probable that "the powers of the gilds had been so much affected by the legislation of Edward VI, that they had but little influence for good or evil." Pt. 1, p. 26.

[2] Professor Cheyney deems this act the heaviest blow inflicted on the gilds by the government, because it deprived them of a considerable portion of their wealth. *Industrial and Social History*, p. 158.

gilds seem to have retained or regained sufficient wealth to warrant the property of the "fraternity, gild, corporation, mystery, brotherhood, company or commonalty," being included among goods assessed for taxes in the general subsidy acts of the sixteenth and seventeenth centuries.[1]

How large a rôle this act really played in the decline of fraternities by eliminating the religious features from craft life, is a matter which can be considered only in passing, in connection with the theory of Mr. Hibbert. He has declared that as a direct result of this enactment, gilds completely changed their nature, and from brotherhoods of workmen "became simply leagues of employers, companies of capitalists."[2] Yet when we remember how the mercers of Shrewsbury, in the by-laws confirmed by the charter of Edward IV, in 1480, attempted to moderate the excessive fines charged apprentices for entry into the gild,—a sign, as Mr. Hibbert himself laments, of a great falling-off from the original spirit of brotherhood,[3]—it appears inconsistent to lay such stress upon this same aspect of craft development at the later period.

Professor Ashley has, we believe, rightly estimated the effects of this measure. According to his view there was no violent break in the continuity of craft-gild development afterwards;[4] and his theory is fully corroborated by the extent of craft activity in the later sixteenth century. Craft gilds are prominent in all parts of the country. Not only are they renewing previous charters,

[1] Professor Ashley has a full discussion in *Eng. Econ. Hist.*, vol. ii, p. 157.

[2] *Influence and Development of Eng. Gilds*, p. 75.

[3] *Ibid.*, pp. 64-5.

[4] *Op. cit.*, p. 155.

but new bodies even as late as Edward's reign are for the first time obtaining recognition. The tailors at Kingston-upon-Hull[1] procure a composition from the municipality, and the skinners and shoemakers obtain letters patent confirming them in their ancient monopoly. In Chester, in the sixth year of Edward's reign, the bakers display letters patent expressly confirming a previous charter of Henry VII.[2]

As an illustration of the importance assigned to commercial interests we may note the incorporation, for the first time, of the merchant companies. In the first year of King Edward, the Governor, Wardens, Assistants and Society of Merchant Venturers of Newcastle were formally incorporated.[3] In 1552 the Merchant Venturers of Bristol obtained a like privilege, upon their representation that "artificers and handicraftsmen having other occupations and without having served an apprenticeship as merchants, exported goods in foreign bottoms, to the defraud of the customs, the scandal of the merchants and the decay of ships and mariners."[4]

During the reign of Mary, the mayor and burgesses of Kingston-upon-Hull granted a set of ordinances to the mystery of "Berbruers" who were in "greate Ruyne and decay."[5] The weavers of Cirencester also record a charter from Philip and Mary.[6] In Liverpool the tailors[7] received a charter upon petition to the city authorities; and in Boston, the cordwainers had their craft regulations sanctioned by the same instrumentality.[8] In

[1] Lambert, *Two Thousand Years*, pp. 236–9.

[2] *Report Historical MSS. Commission*, vol. viii, p. 402.

[3] Gross, *Gild Merchant*, vol. ii, p. 385.

[4] Hunt, *Bristol*, p. 134.

[5] Lambert, *op. cit.*, p. 223.

[6] *Trans. Bristol and Glouc. Arch. Soc.*, vol. viii, p. 184.

[7] Walford, *Gilds*, p. 147.

[8] *Ibid.*, p. 158.

1554, the Merchant Adventurers of Chester[1] received a crown charter with the usual powers, which however were not to prejudice either the rights of the crown, the laws of the land or the privileges of the mayor.

The statute book yields plentiful evidence of the continuance of craft gilds, for example in the act prescribing that "countrymen shall only be permitted to retail goods in corporate towns . . . when they shall be free of the gilds and liberties of the said cities and boroughs."[2]

2. *Policy of the Elizabethan Government. Statute of Apprentices.*—With the reign of Elizabeth, records of craft organization and of gild activity become increasingly abundant. Yet that period also has sometimes been regarded as the time when the system received its death-blow by the passage of the great act of 1563,[3] the celebrated Statute of Apprentices. Why so disastrous an effect upon so well-grounded a system could be expected from the re-enactment of a statute of laborers, such as had figured upon the statute book for two centuries, has by no means been made clear by adherents of that interesting theory, and a detailed study of the act in its relation to the craft-gild system has failed to corroborate their view.

This statute of apprentices was an exceedingly detailed and comprehensive piece of legislation, embodying the best action up to that time taken on the question of labor and its accompanying problems. The object was clearly expressed in the preamble. The industrial world was in a chaotic state, due, it was supposed, to the countless number of statutes which from the time of the Black Death had attempted to adjust the wages of labor to social

[1] Gross, *op. cit.*, vol. ii, pp. 360–2.

[2] 1 and 2 Philip and Mary, c. 7.

[3] 5 Elizabeth, c. 4.

conditions.[1] Many of these acts, says the preamble, were now imperfect and contrary, and not answerable to the changes which had led to an advance in the prices of commodities. The situation entailed great grief and burden upon the poor laborer, and called for relief. Hence this act of Elizabeth proposed to take the substance of the best existing statutes and combine them into one comprehensive measure to cure the existing ills of the laborer in husbandry as well as in the arts and crafts, and to give them all in times, whether of "plentie" or "scarcitee," a convenient proportion of wages.

It is important to note first of all that the government by its own declaration contemplated no serious innovation. The numerous acts previously passed to regulate wages were no longer adequate to meet the needs of a more advanced social development. Therefore, Parliament, to cure certain obvious industrial ills, proposed simply to take "the substance of as many of the said laws as are meet to be continued," and to combine them into one statute, hoping so to bring order into the industrial chaos. The provisions of the act had in fact figured upon the statute-book more or less, from the date of the earliest statute of laborers.[2]

[1] The statute was re-enacted with slight variations thirteen times within the succeeding century. See Cheyney, *op. cit.*, pp. 107–9 for a list of these repetitions.

[2] Although the conclusions here presented were reached before the appearance of the new edition of Professor Cunningham's *Modern Times*, much of the new material therein contained or referred to serves to corroborate them. For example, an interesting letter to Cecil dated September 3, 1562, shows what serious consideration the government was giving to social problems. It also indicates the attitude of the public toward state interference in economic affairs. It represents the situation in the same light as the preamble. Mr. Hewins, in his article "The Regulation of Wages by the Justice of the Peace," *Economic Journal*, vol. viii, p. 342, publishes this letter.

Only a few articles in this elaborate industrial code need special consideration here—those concerned with the assessment of wages, with the formulation of a stated term for apprentice service, and with the appointment of authorities to provide for the enforcement of the measure. The last point requires special emphasis in this connection, since it has never before been taken into account in discussions of the bearing of this important statute upon the gilds. The clauses will be treated chiefly with reference to the theories of previous writers upon craft organizations, since a study of conditions subsequent to the act has failed to bear out many assertions heretofore advanced.

Professor Ashley, in tracing the lines of development of craft history in the second half of the sixteenth century, emphasizes the fact that this act of Elizabeth transferred to the justices of the peace or to the chief officers of the boroughs, acting as justices, almost the whole of the jurisdiction over journeymen and apprentices, and that above all it bestowed on them, in preference to the governing bodies of the crafts, the power to fix the wages of journeymen.[1] From this interpretation one might infer that the measure introduced for the first time the jurisdiction of the justices of the peace into the crafts, and, far more important, that it assigned to them for the first time the duty of apportioning the wages to be paid by craft masters to their employees. If such innovations could be proved, the government could be credited with a measure far more important than its own announcement of its intentions would warrant us in anticipating, and with alterations in craft organizations, which, to judge by its policy as expressed in other

[1] *Eng. Econ. Hist.*, vol. ii, pp. 159-160.

measures intended for the benefit of the system, it neither contemplated nor desired.

As a basis for the criticism of this view of the act, we must first consider the character of former methods of assessing wages. To whom since the rise of the gild system had the determination of the wage of labor been entrusted?

1. *Assessment of Wages.*—A consideration of this question demands a review of the industrial situation at least from the Norman period. We see that as early as Henry II's day occasional social upheavals took place, and that any derangement in social conditions brought other attendant changes which provoked national or local intervention. The first instance of this kind was a local disaster in London, probably a fire,[1] that produced a rise in wages which the London authorities attempted to stay by fixing the sum to be paid to men engaged in the building trades. During the thirteenth century scales of wages for those trades were several times drawn up by city officers. This practice was continued under Edward I, and applied not only to the building trades[2] but to others, notably the blacksmiths

[1] Bateson, *Mediaeval England*, p. 267. "In 1212 master carpenters, masons and tilers got 3 d., their servers, 1½ d., free-stone carvers, 2½ d., plasterers and daubers, diggers and sievers somewhat less, per day; all received food in addition, or 1½ d., in its stead." *Ibid.*, p. 268.

[2] In the early part of his reign carpenters, masons, plasterers, tilers and daubers mostly received wages on a similar scale. Between Michaelmas and Martinmas they had 4 d. per day, or else 1½ d. and their table at the option of the employed; between Martinmas and the Purification, 3 d., or 1 d. and their table. Between the Purification and Easter, 4 d., or 1½ d. and their table. Servants' wages were also designated and penalty for infringement of these rules was provided. *Liber Albus*. Introduction, xxxvi.

as well.[1] In the reign of Edward III, the leather trades appeared to need royal intervention, and special writs specified the punishment to be inflicted upon skinners, saddlers and tanners for excessive charges.[2]

But whereas incidents such as these were largely the result of special local disturbances, the wide confusion in the industrial world resulting from "the great pestilence" made the regulation of the wage of labor a national concern, and evoked the first of that series of legislative acts known as the statutes of laborers. The government in a spirit of conservatism lent the weight of its authority toward checking changes already in progress, and ruled that "no one was to pay or to promise to pay more than was customary in the twentieth year" of this reign,[3] that is, before the ravages of the plague had unsettled the social economy. Mayors and bailiffs, moreover, were empowered to inquire into breaches of the law. London, not slow to take advantage of new rights in the same year began to regulate wages within its limits "to amend and redress grievances which the good folks of the city, rich and poor, have suffered within the past year because all manner of labourers take immeasurably more than they have been wont to take."[4]

The action of some of the London craft gilds is suggestive in this connection. In 1350[5] the city authorities, by command of the king, examined conditions in the shearmens' trade, and "set down for certain what they shall take for each piece of work." The shearmen expressed themselves as satisfied with the estimates, "if only they may have their servants and journeymen at the same wages

[1] They were to have 1½ d. for putting on a common horse-shoe with six nails, and 2 d. for one with eight nails. *Ibid.*, liii.

[2] *Ibid.*, liv.

[3] 23 Edward III, c. 5.

[4] Riley, *Memorials of London*, p. 253.

[5] *Ibid.*, p. 250.

that they used to have," and went on to petition that the said servingmen be chastised and commanded under certain penalty, to work according to ancient usage. In 1380 the cutlers appeared before the civic authorities with certain articles which they asked to have enrolled in the Chamber, that in time to come they might be better observed. Prominent among those was a provision forbidding the payment of excessive wages to journeymen, an evil to prevent which overseers were to be sworn to award wages according to their consciences.[1]

In Bristol, as early as 1347, the wage question required treatment by the gilds. It is interesting to note there the extent of their reliance upon civic authorities. The fullers in ordinances "newly made before the mayor, recorder and other good men there assembled," named the wages that masters should pay their workmen, or be subject to a fine for infringement. Furthermore, to maintain these articles, six men were elected by the mayor, and sworn before him with the understanding that if any member should feel himself aggrieved by the conduct of these six, the mayor should make amendment.[2] In 1364 the cobblers[3] appealed to the city officials for relief, being "well nigh impoverished by the excessive price of their servants, who are loath to be attendant to the said craft unless they have too outrageous and excessive salary, contrary to the statute of our lord the King and the usages of the said town." Town ordinances of the period determined also what the tailors were to take for the cutting and making of a robe.

[1] Riley, *op. cit.*, p. 438.

[2] *Little Red Book*, vol. ii, p. 10.

[3] *Ibid.*, p. 41.

[4] *Ibid.*, vol. ii, p. 31. "It is ordained that the tailors of the town shall not in future take for the cutting and making of a robe more than 18 d., under penalty of 40 d., so that the aforesaid tailors shall find thread, buckram and silk for the lining of the sleeves."

Toward the end of the fourteenth century, as we are aware, a new set of officials became a permanent part of the national administrative and judicial machinery. Legislative acts from the time of Richard II gave them particular authority in the rating of wages. As an act of the period has it, "because a man cannot put the price of corn and other victuals in certain," justices of the peace in their sessions were to make proclamation "by their discretion, how much every mason, carpenter, tiler and other craftsmen, workmen and other laborers shall take by the day, with or without meat and drink."[1] The assessment of the rate of wages was thus a matter for frequent adjustment through the government, and its officials were invested with authority to pronounce upon the question.

Throughout the following century, legislative enactments continued to fix rates of wages with some variation in the method of procedure. Sometimes an act itself determined the amount of wages for various kinds of labor, giving justices merely the power of enforcement.[2] Occasionally it gave those officials power both of assessment and of enforcement.[3] Actual records, moreover, show that justices carried out the provisions. From an early register still extant in Norfolk we gather that in the ninth year of Henry VI,[4] justices of the peace in that county were fixing the wages to be paid a large number of artisans and laborers in rural districts.

[1] 13 Richard II, Stat. 1, c. 8.

[2] 2 Henry V, Stat. 1, c. 4. 23 Henry VI, c. 12.

[3] 2 Henry VI, c. 18, gave justices power to assess wages as well.

[4] This is a register in the manors of the Hundred and a half of Mitford, belonging to the Bishop of Ely, and shows the justices rating the wages for the plowmen, shepherds, carters, maltesters, for a woman servant of husbandry; for a dycher, waller, hegger, dawber, a baylly of husbandrye, for masons, leyers, reders, tilers, carpenters and sawers. *Eng. Hist. Rev.*, vol. xiii, p. 300.

But within the boroughs the methods of the fourteenth century persisted throughout the fifteenth. In London a charter to the fullers and shearmen ordered that no householder should give wages to any apprentice "newly out of his time," until he should be presented to the master and wardens, and he was then "to take wages according to custom."[1] Ordinances of the Bristol fullers, confirmed in 1406 before the civic officials, provided that masters should not give their men more than a stated sum.[2] In 1424 the town authorities of Coventry interfered in the weavers' craft with an ordinance for a regular wage.[3] In Worcester a city regulation of 1497 significantly prescribed that "no carpenter ne mason take more by the day than the lawe wult, upon peyn of punishment according to the statute therefore late made and provided."[4]

In the early sixteenth century an enactment of Henry VIII's Parliament determined the scale of wages and gave justices of the peace jurisdiction over offenders.[5] Here again London records furnish evidence of the method of enforcing such acts. The aldermen were instructed to summon artificers before them and to ascertain what wages masters were giving to their workmen. Then they were to command them to "geve ne take more nor

[1] Herbert, *Twelve Great Livery Cos.*, vol. ii, p. 656.

[2] *Little Red Book*, vol. ii, p. 75. "The masters of the craft aforesaid shall not give more to the labourers of the said craft than four pence a day, the penalty to the masters to be two shillings on every occasion, 12, d. to the commonalty and 12, d. to the craft." "And if the men are rebels and will not work," then the masters were to have power to take them before the mayor to be dealt with according to law and reason.

[3] Harris, *Life in an Old Eng. Town*, p. 277.

[4] Green, *History of Worcester*, vol. ii. Appendix, xlix.

[5] 6 Henry VIII, c. 3.

greater wages than in the last statute of our said souer-aigne lord the VI yere of his Reigne is lymyted."[1] From that time the London common council seems to concern itself more closely with the wage question. In 1521 it appointed a committee of members from different companies to assess wages in the builders' trades. Again in 1538 it regulated by ordinance both the hours of work and the amount of wages for laborers and handicraftsmen. After 1490 the municipality of Coventry interfered in the cappers' trade, chiefly at first to prescribe the length of the working day.[2] In 1520 and again in 1526 the same authority found it necessary to assert itself, ordering the masters to curtail the wages paid to their men unless they adhered to the stated hours. In Southampton the wardens of the shearmen complained in 1504 to the mayor of disobedience to the rules of their craft and "it was agreed that the shearmen should take for the takkyng and foldyng for every kersey a half penny."[3]

Summarizing then this account of the methods by which from the beginning wages had been regulated, we find that up to the middle of the fourteenth century, the question was left for local municipal adjustment. Under Edward III, however, it began to engage the attention of crown and parliament. Both royal writ and parliamentary statute treated of the rates of wages. The first statute of laborers marks an epoch in the English industrial world although constant reiteration and various additions were necessary to accomplish real results. Upon the institution of the office of justice of the peace, that official received jurisdiction in the matter of wages and evidently performed his duties at least to the extent

[1] *Eng. Hist. Review*, vol. xv, pp. 449-50.

[2] Harris, *op. cit.*, p. 279.

[3] Davies, *Southampton*, 271.

of settling the rates to be paid in his locality. Within the boroughs civic authorities continued to adjust differences upon the subject of wages between masters and men and to determine by ordinance the proper rates to be paid. Deference was universally paid by the crafts to the superior power of the municipality.[1] Borough endorsement was procured to enable craft dignitaries to enforce craft rulings upon their members. Up to 1563, therefore, it seems apparent that in rural districts the justices of the peace, and in cities and boroughs the municipal officers furnished, as a rule, the authority for the ultimate settlement of all questions regarding wages.

To return to the provision of the act of 1563 concerning the assessment of wages, which, according to Professor Ashley introduced into the industrial world the innovation of the jurisdiction of the justice of the peace, we read that justices of the peace in every shire, the sheriff in the counties, and every mayor, bailiff or other head officer within any city or corporate town are yearly to limit, rate and appoint wages, after consultation with some of the discreet and grave persons of their neighborhood about the "plentie or scarcitie" of the season.[2] There seems to be no great novelty in this arrangement. We have certainly heard before that the justices of the peace in the counties and the mayors or head officers in the boroughs assessed the wages of labor. We have not, however, observed before that this was to be done

[1] Mr. Hutchins, in discussing the question of the regulation of wages, concludes that while the "nature and amount of the control exercised by the town authorities . . . cannot be very precisely defined," yet the most usual plan "seems to have been a mutual arrangement between the gild and the town." "The Regulation of Wages by Gilds and Town Authorities." *Economic Journal*, vol. x, p. 404.

[2] 5 Elizabeth, c. 4, sect. xi.

by consultation with some of the discreet persons of their neighborhood. Has the phrase any significance? We note also that there is here no confining of jurisdiction to the justices of the peace, but that borough magistrates are to have like authority to execute the regulation within borough limits.

Borough procedure after 1563 shows that the city officials so understood the new provisions. Immediately upon this legislation the lord mayor of London and "all the residue of the justices of the peace" met "for the stallynge and ratynge of the wages of artyficers and laborers according to the Acte."[1] A later record states that "the rates of artyfycers servauntes and laborers wages taxed ye last yere accordinge to the statute . . . within ye cytye of London were this daye ratyfyed confirmed and alowed by ye lorde mayre and ye rest of ye Justices of ye peace . . . to remayne stande and be observid for ye yere insuynge." Again in 1573,

vpon complaynt hereafter to be made to any lord maior by any persone or persones that cannot get ainny laboringe man of any occupaçon what so euer that will worke for suche wage as is appoynted and sessed by my lord maior . . . then my lord maior shall at his pleasor appoynt suche forrens as shall pleas his lordshippe: And to punyshe the offendors.[2]

[1] This is recorded in the "repertory," the book of the Court of Aldermen. They probably rated wages in their capacity of justices of the peace but entered their rulings in the aldermen's records. *Eng. Hist. Review*, vol. xv. p. 451.

[2] *Ibid.*, p. 453. The Mayor and Justices of Kingston-upon-Hull in 1570 issued a proclamation of wages. "We the aforesaid Mayor and Justices have limited, rated and assessed the wages in manner and form aforesaid, for that it seemeth to divers discreet and sage men of the said town and county, whose advice and opinions we have taken herein that the same is most convenient both to the giver and taker." See Cunningham, *Modern Times*, pt. i, p. 39.

In London therefore the mayor and aldermen promptly took entire charge of the rating of wages in accordance with the provisions of the statutes. In Liverpool,[1] the city records of 1592 show the municipality dictating the rate of wages. "Noe workman or labourer at husbandry or other labour shall take for his or their day wag above three pence between Michaelmas and Candlemas."

In general the same methods had been employed to regulate wages as to determine prices. Indeed the latter problem had been from early times intimately connected with the wage question as indicated in the first statute of laborers. The English government did not recognize the craft gilds as a prime authority in settling either. Final decision in times of crisis it reserved for itself, delegating ordinary power first to the municipal authorities, who had exercised it from the start, and later to the justices of the peace throughout the shires of the realm. After the town magnates had been likewise invested with powers of justices they possessed added authority for the exercise of this particular function. London records certainly suggest that the regulation of the wage of labor engaged their attention.

That the craft gilds, moreover, admitted the existence of this power in the municipality, and that they yielded it at least nominal obedience is proved by their frequent application to borough officials for endorsement of craft by-laws whenever the question of wages is mentioned. Professor Ashley, indeed, cites two examples to show the exercise of the right of fixing wages by the gild; but a careful reading of the ordinances quoted leaves one still extremely doubtful as to whether the gilds ever

[1] Picton, *Liverpool*, p. 113. In 1594 this regulation was repeated with the further proviso that "from Candlemas to Michaelmas the wages shall be four pence the day and not above."

really ventured so far by their own authority. One of Mr. Ashley's illustrations is a rule of the London cutlers already referred to,[1] who in 1380 applied to the city officials for the endorsement and enrollment of that and their other by-laws, that they might be better observed in the future.[2] The other example is taken from the court of the London carpenters in the sixteenth century, where "by my lord mayor's commandment the carpenters waygs was rated yf they dyd fynd themselves meat and drynke at xiiii d. the day and their servants xii d."[3] This last example might be taken as significant evidence of the mayor's authority. It is not clear, therefore, on

[1] *Supra*, p. 93.

[2] This by-law reads as follows: "To provide against the excessive wages of the journeymen of the said trade, be it ordained that no journeyman work in the same, who is not free . . . or who has not served seven years within the city in such trade shall be admitted to work in the same, if such journeyman have not first been tried by the overseers, sworn in the trade as to his knowledge therein, to ascertain how much he is deserving to take by the day, by the week, or for a whole term; and as they shall find, according to their consciences, that such journeymen can well serve, let them award him what he is to take. . ." This would seem to be a general provision to determine the ability of journeymen, and within certain limits the manner of their payment. There is nothing to show that the gild named the rates of wages of their workmen as a whole. Riley, *op. cit.*, p. 439.

[3] Jupp and Pocock, *Carpenters Company*, p. 379. One case has been found where a craft gild, apparently without any municipal authorization set about "assessing" wages. In 1551 the London barbers show an order in their Court Minutes, which provides that no barber was to take a "foreigner" and set him to work without presenting him to the master and wardens, and that the masters were to "sess" the wages for such "foreigners," according to their ability, xii d. a week, x d. or as the masters should think "meate and convenyente." In this case, the emphasis laid upon the word foreigners suggests that this was perhaps an exceptional and urgent case, calling for unusual action. This interpretation seems justified moreover. by the comment of the editor, that many foreigners who were inexpert had at that time come to the city. See *Annals of the Barber-Surgeons*, p. 171.

what grounds Professor Ashley maintains that the craft gilds were seriously affected by this great statute of Elizabeth, since records depict practically the same procedure in the method of determining wages after the enactment as before. Gild by-laws never lay claim to any independent prerogative in the matter.

On the other hand, while there is nothing absolutely new in the provision giving justices of the peace jurisdiction in the assessment of wages, the clause which calls for their consultation with some of the discreet men of the neighborhood may be significant. Who would these discreet men be, and whom would they be inclined to favor, craft masters or men? This question finds an answer in a document of the early seventeenth century. Despite the comprehensiveness of the act of 1563 labor difficulties still cropped up requiring new consideration. In the very first year of the reign of James I,[1] a bill was passed which attempted to explain the ambiguity of the provision relating to the assessment of wages. An order issued in London in compliance with this later act summoning a meeting of the justices of the peace, prescribes that "the wardens of the Companies of such Artificers within this Cittye as are within the meaning of that statute shalbe warned to be there present before the sayd justices."[2] Clearly the wardens of the craft gilds are the discreet men consulted by the justices in regard to wages. The influence of the gilds is certainly in evidence.[3]

[1] 1 James I, c. 6. [2] *Eng. Hist. Review*, vol. xv, p. 454.

[3] The master and wardens of the "Companie of Carpenters" complying with the request of the Lord Mayor of London asking their advice concerning wages drew up a scale in 1655, "for the reducing of the excessive wages of laborers and workemen in these times of great plenty" which they "humbly conceive to be sufficient." See "The Regulation of Wages by Gilds and Town Authorities." *Economic Journal*, vol. x, p. 406.

Still another question arises as we attempt to measure the influence of this statute upon the gild system. Even granting that the provisions instituted novel methods of industrial procedure, taking from the gilds certain valuable earlier powers, we still have to decide how far the Elizabethan government was able to enforce its legislation, and so how far state action can really be counted a hostile factor in the decay of the gild system. Here too the act of James above mentioned is of aid. After reciting the act of Elizabeth, it continues:

Whereas the said Act hath not, according to the true meaning thereof, been duly put in execution, whereby the rates of wages for poor artificers . . . whose wages was meant to be rated . . . have not been rated and proportioned according to the plenty, scarcity, and necessity and respect of the time which was politicly intended . . . by reason that ambiguity and question have arisen and been made, whether the rating of all manner of artificers . . . should or might be rated by the said law,

therefore it is needful to define the limits within which the regulation shall hold good.

Obviously the earlier act had not been altogether clear to the authorities entrusted with its enforcement.[1] A wide latitude had been possible for its interpreters, militating against any rigid insistence upon its execution,

[1] It appears too that there were many complaints of failure on the part of the justices of the peace to exercise the power of inquiry into the rates of wages which had been bestowed upon them by the act. This power was "omitted in all places and the rather because there is no clarke or register appoynted to attend upon them. . . This is thinge that is not done in moste places, and therefore the statute remayneth utterly unobservede, as if there were no such lawe at all." Cunningham, "The Perversion of Economic History." *Economic Journal*, vol. ii, p. 300, note 3.

and therefore against its influence upon the gild system. All evidence therefore tends simply to prove that we cannot safely argue any serious effects from this Elizabethan provision upon the welfare of the craft gilds. There was nothing novel in the nomination of the justice of the peace to determine the rate of wages, nor were the terms of the statute so clearly expressed as to admit of a uniform and undisputed enforcement. Unquestionably, moreover, the gilds transgressed this law as they had transgressed others which we have noticed heretofore. Otherwise there would have been no steady complaints of non-enforcement, and no repetition of acts aiming at the correction of the same class of offences.

2. *Seven Years' Term of Apprenticeship.*—The most interesting portion of the great statute connected with the craft-gild system is perhaps that which defines the period of apprenticeship, the first general definition of the kind by national legislation. To quote the wording of the statute: "Householders in cities and corporate towns may take in any art or mystery or manual occupation . . . the son of any freeman not occupying husbandry nor being a laborer to serve and be bound as an apprentice after the custom and order of the city of London for seven years at the least . . . "[1] Again, "It shall not be lawful to any persons other than such as now do lawfully use or exercise any art, mystery or manual occupation to set up and occupy, use or exercise any craft . . . or occupation, except that he shall have been brought up therein seven years at least as apprentice."[2] Here accordingly are articles of considerable importance in a study of governmental policy toward the gild system. What is the significance of the insertion of such

[1] 5 Elizabeth, c. 4, sect. xix. [2] *Ibid.*, sect. xxiv.

provisions at this time in a statute of laborers? What had been the requirements for apprenticeship throughout the previous centuries of the existence of the gilds?

The act itself refers to the city of London as a place where the custom was in force.[1] With this allusion as a guide we find the earliest traces of the practice of apprenticeship among London records. The first extant notice of it seems to be in some customs proclaimed in the time of Edward I, to the effect "that no person shall from henceforth receive an apprentice if he be not himself free of the city . . . and that no apprentice shall be received for a less term than seven years, according to the ancient and established usage."[2] How long this usage had been in vogue, or when first it had been introduced into English industrial life we have no means of knowing. Nor can we tell when it was first applied to gild labor. London records show only that by the middle of the fourteenth century the rule held a prominent place in craft by-laws within the city. In 1344 the girdlers made the seven years' service a prerequisite to membership in the craft. In 1345 the spurriers included the same requirement among their regulations. In 1350 the shearmen followed the example and other trades were not far behind.

In Bristol as we have seen,[3] an apprenticeship was first demanded by the barbers in 1418, by the hoopers in 1439.[4] In Shrewsbury, a similar provision had a place

[1] Just when apprenticeship service appeared in England is not known. It probably came into general use during the reign of Henry III, for apprentices are mentioned in records of the reign of Edward I. Norton, *Commentaries*, p. 106.

[2] Riley, *Memorials of London*, p. 247. [3] *Introduction, supra*, p. 30.

[4] *Little Red Book*, vol. ii, pp. 137, 163.

in the charter conferred by Henry VI upon the barbers.[1] In Kingston-upon-Hull there is no sign of such an institution until 1490 and 1499, when the by-laws of the weavers and the glovers order its adoption.[2] In Newcastle the rule was comprised among the saddlers' ordinances in 1459.[3] In the sixteenth century, the seven-years apprenticeship was a feature of the merchant adventurers in Chester[4] and in Bristol.[5] It was prescribed by a town ordinance in Worcester in 1467.[6] Thus by the end of the fifteenth century a uniform term of apprenticeship for craft membership was a practically universal custom, supported by both municipal and gild authority.

Nor is this the first time that the seven-years term is mentioned in an act of Parliament. A statute of Henry VII,[7] had required the Norwich shearers to serve such an apprenticeship. When the government of Edward VI issued its regulations for the manufacture of woolen cloth throughout the realm, it ordered that no one should weave unless he had "bene an apprentice to the occupacon . . . for the space of seven yeres at the least."[8] The Weavers' act of 1555 also demanded the same qualification for entrance to that craft, the northern counties alone being exempt from the decree.[9]

[1] Hibbert, *Inf. and Develop. of English Gilds*, p. 64.

[2] Lambert, *Two Thousand Years*, pp. 205, 216.

[3] Brand, *History and Antiquities of Newcastle*, vol. ii, p. 317.

[4] Gross, *Gild Merchant*, vol. ii, pp. 360–2. [5] *Ibid.*, p. 355.

[6] Smith, *Eng. Gilds*, p. 390.

[7] 11 Henry VII, c. 10, 11.

[8] 5 and 6 Edward VI, c. 8. The act nominated the persons who should weave or make broad woollen cloths. C. 24 provided the same requirement for the manufacture of hats and coverlets at Norwich.

[9] 2 and 3 Philip and Mary, c. 11.

Nevertheless special significance attaches to the first appearance of the stated term of apprenticeship in a general statute of laborers like the act of 1563. In introducing this regulation into the labor world at large, the English government gave a national character to a custom which had been first enforced only by the city of London and thence adopted into gild constitutions in various parts of the country. As a feature of industrial life it had become of prime importance through centuries of usage. Indeed, as we have seen, the barbers of Bristol had appealed to the city authorities for permission to insert a provision of the sort among their by-laws, in order to keep their craft from utter destruction. They looked to it as a means to avert the competition of non-members. Some recognition of the value of the institution of apprenticeship in industrial life apparently induced the government to put it on a national basis and incorporate the clauses regarding it in the statute of laborers.

Yet Mr. Hibbert, when considering this act in its relation to the gild system, sees in it simply a blow aimed directly at craft organizations. Their functions, he says, were now taken over by the government; consequently many gilds came to an end, while others were amalgamated into one or two larger and amended corporations.[1] This is a surprising statement in view both of what has gone before, and of what is yet to be related of the situation. What functions, we ask, were taken away from the craft gilds? We have already demonstrated that the justices of the peace in fixing the rates of wages were not depriving them of any earlier powers. Was the government now invading their right to decide the

[1] *Influence and Develop. of Eng. Gilds*, p. 83.

length of their own apprenticeships, long one of their most important privileges? On the contrary, it would seem that, by insisting upon a customary term, the government was showing itself thoroughly in sympathy with the policy pursued by the associations and was giving them distinct encouragement to continue.

This view, moreover, is corroborated by a consideration of the provisions for the enforcement of the act.

3. *Authorities Appointed to Enforce the Act of 1563.*—Section xxx of the act of 1563 ordained that

> the justices of the peace of every county, dividing themselves into several limits, and likewise every mayor and head officer of any city or town corporate, shall yearly . . . by all such ways and means as to their wisdoms shall be thought most meet, make a special and diligent inquiry of the branches and articles of this statute and of the good execution of the same. . . .

When we remember that craft gilds existed chiefly in boroughs and corporate towns, under the jurisdiction of municipal authorities, who acted also as justices of the peace, and that relations between those officials and the gilds were necessarily intimate in the interests of both town and craft, we can but ask, who, if not craft authorities, could see that this apprenticeship requirement, now become a part of national law, was enforced? Who else was in a position to do so? Who else had been enforcing such a regulation from the time of its first appearance in English industrial life? Indeed, the need of enforcing it had been one motive to call craft organization into existence.

Yet the further question arises, why was the provision now inserted in a statute of laborers? Is there any connection between its appearance and the industrial changes which had been going on for at least a century—the rise of the so-called "domestic system," and the spread of industries into country districts away from chartered towns and gild supervision? Regarded in this light, would not the insertion of an apprenticeship clause in an act of Parliament be a triumph for the gild system? Moreover, is there anything to show that in cases where artisans refused to be bound by the regulation it was ever enforced by any other agency than the craft gilds?[1] When the borough authorities commissioned to enforce this measure were fain to rely upon craft organizations for aid, how would or could it be rigidly executed in rural districts whenever masters or men were deliberately bent upon neglecting it? In spite of lax enforcement,[2]

[1] For example, in 1578 an action was brought before the mayor and sheriffs of Nottingham at the instance of three townsmen against a worker in iron "being then and yet a person other than such as lawfully used or exercised" the occupation of ironmonger. He was charged with never having served a seven years' apprenticeship. One cannot but question whether the accusers were not ironmongers and so themselves materially interested in upholding the monopoly of their craft. *Nottingham Records*, vol. iv, p. 51.

[2] Mr. Cunningham some time ago called attention to the fact that "the working of the apprenticeship clauses of the Act of 1563 was a subject of complaint in 1573" when it "gave rise to an inquiry which resulted in the drafting of amending measures." These, however, were dropped before definite action had been taken upon them. Mr. Cunningham uses this incident as an argument to strengthen the view which he expresses in the earlier edition of his *Growth of English Industry and Commerce*, that "these complaints throw light on the circumstances which brought about the formation or revival of companies among the crafts in Elizabeth's reign." *Economic Journal*, vol. ii, p. 300, note 3. According to this view the absence of provision in the statute of 1563 for supervising the quality of wares led to the organization of companies which in his opinion "somewhat resembled and occasionally really continued the old craft companies." Vol. ii, p. 45, 1890 edition. In the new edition of his work, Mr. Cunningham still maintains this view of the revival of the gild system under Elizabeth. To quote his own words, "The desirability of obtaining some machinery for enforcing this enact-

however, the very fact of the incorporation of an apprenticeship rule in the act at a time when the government was still engaged in prohibiting the spread of industries from corporate towns, as it had been since 1465,[1] was a triumph for the gild system and an encouragement of their methods against those of the newer industrial organizations.

We next turn to Professor Ashley's interpretation of the place of this act in the government's industrial policy. According to him, the government looking out upon the industries under the gild system felt the need of bringing them more closely under public control, and drew up the clauses of this statute of apprentices to confer added jurisdiction on the justices of the peace. Hence followed a certain weakening of the gild system.[2] Why, however,

ment would appear to have been one of the reasons which led to the resuscitation of industrial companies in the latter years of Elizabeth's reign. These companies were different in many ways from the craft gilds, even when they were erected upon their ruins." *Modern Times*, pt. 1, p. 35. Mr. Hibbert holds a similar theory of the reorganization of the gild system under Elizabeth. Yet do not such views argue an imperfect conception of the natural development of institutions? Are they apt to dissolve and immediately reorganize? The theory of social evolution admits of no such sudden endings and beginnings. We prefer to regard craft history as a constant progressive development. From unobtrusive local associations the gilds gradually transformed themselves into corporations of practically unlimited powers. As we have already shown, the articles of the London Merchant Taylors in 1507 and in 1613 were practically identical. The same continuity appears in gilds everywhere, even in Mr. Hibbert's Shrewsbury companies. He quotes entries of the mercers of "cessments for renewing the composition," in different years of the seventeenth century. *Influence and Develop.*, p. 84.

[1] 4 Edward IV, c. 11, indicated the spread of the system by that time. Legislation under Philip and Mary by acts 2 and 3 Philip and Mary, c. 11; 4 and 5 Phil. and Mary, c. 5, sect. 21, as well as under Elizabeth, as, 1 Eliz., c. 14; 18 Eliz., c. 16, continued to legislate in the interest of corporate towns.

[2] *Eng. Econ. Hist.*, vol. ii, p. 166.

have we not an equal right to say that the government, looking upon the domestic system and upon the industries growing up with no organization, felt the need of bringing them more closely under public control, and conferred special jurisdiction over them upon the justices of the peace as officers whose position the state thought expedient to emphasize?

Mr. Hibbert, less conservative than Professor Ashley, maintains, as we have said, that the act of 1563 introduced a radical change in gild organizations, that, as a result, some gilds came to an end, while others were forced to amalgamate. Precisely what organizations Mr. Hibbert had in mind as coming to an end, for lack of functions to perform, does not appear. On the contrary, in the material he himself uses in illustrating his theory, craft gilds certainly appear to be continuing their work quite as before the passage of the noxious act. Indeed, to use his own words, a composition granted by Elizabeth, in 1564, within a year of this enactment, to the Shrewsbury glovers was quite "as strict as any mediæval regulation."[1] The Shrewsbury crafts enjoy their old powers as fully after 1564 as before. The London gilds also proceed along their former lines. The carpenters pass regulations for their apprentices just as they had been accustomed.[2] The ironmongers formulate rules for the sale of their commodities.[3] The Merchant Taylors appoint suitable persons to see that their craftsmen use a proper yard measure.[4] The goldsmiths bring complaints against their wardens before the mayor.[5]

[1] *Influence and Develop. of Eng. Gilds*, p. 87.

[2] Jupp and Pocock, *Carpenters Company*, p. 363.

[3] Nichols, *Ironmongers*, p. 89.

[4] Herbert, *Twelve Great Livery Companies*, vol. i, p. 47.

[5] *Acts of the Privy Council*, 1575-77, p. 186.

In Kingston-upon-Hull the weavers prepare new craft ordinances during the year after 1563.[1] The cordwainers and other companies as well are seemingly in full operation. Among the Newcastle crafts,[2] the cordwainers in 1566, the cooks in 1575, the millers in 1578, the carpenters in 1579, and the masons in 1581, are drawing up fresh by-laws. Indeed the cooks seem to have secured for the first time the ratification of their by-laws by the city authorities. The Bristol weavers were still doing business in 1602 subservient to the city officials.[3] In Norwich the goldsmiths asked the mayor, aldermen and council for ordinances "for that no good orders and constitucons have ben hetherto made and provided for the dewe investigacon and searche of abuses."[4] The Boston tailors display considerable activity, entering by-laws on three different occasions between 1562 and 1575.[5] In Chester a municipal charter was issued to the weavers as one of that city's ancient companies.[6] In Winchester likewise many craft-gild records of the period are preserved. The ordinances of the shoemakers and cobblers drawn up in 1580 reveal a state of affairs worthy of special mention. They demand that the seven-years apprenticeship should be observed because many unpractised in those trades had established themselves in Winchester, and faulty shoes were made and sold to the hurt and deception of the city.[7] From this survey we conclude that craft gilds had not yet lost their vigor nor ceased to perform their functions, notwithstanding the Elizabethan act of 1563.

[1] Lambert, *op. cit.*, pp. 207, 315. [2] Brand, *op. cit.*, pp. 317, 346.

[3] *Annals of Bristol*, 17th Century, p. 17.

[4] *Reliquary*, New Series, vol. iv, p. 208. [5] Thompson, *Boston*, p. 158.

[6] *Report Historical MSS. Commission*, vol. viii, p. 402.

[7] Walford, *op. cit.*, p. 128.

This conclusion is again confirmed by frequent mentions of craft organizations in statutory legislation. Examples, moreover, furnished by Mr. Hibbert from the Shrewsbury records prove unmistakably that the Elizabethan government was often quite ready to help craft gilds in their effort to retain their former powers. The Shrewsbury drapers presented an address containing a pitiful tale of disorders in their borough because unskilled men bought defectively-made cloth, to the decay of their trade and the loss of the poor shearmen. In response, the company was given sole right to buy all the Welsh cloth brought into their city.[1] But a few years later the attention of the government was again called to conditions in Shrewsbury, where the desired enactment had not brought about the expected good results, but had rather resulted in "the impoverishing and undoing of the poore artificers and others at whose Suite the said Acte was procured." Accordingly, the injurious act was repealed, for the good of the city.[2] However, the incident illustrates the harmony between the gilds and the government, and the acquiescence of the latter in craft requests.[3]

[1] By act of 8 Eliz. c. 7, "divers artificers and other persons within the said town, not of the said company or mystery . . . who have of late with great disorder upon a mere covetous desire occupied the said trade . . . having no knowledge, experience, or skill in the same, by reason whereof they buy defective cloth not truly made . . . whereby the said trade is greatly decayed and discredited, to the great loss and hindrance of the poor shearmen . . . who were wont to be set on work thereby."

[2] 14 Eliz., c. 12.

[3] Why Mr. Hibbert ascribes this legislation for Shrewsbury to state purposes in which a special use was made of the Shrewsbury drapers does not seem clear. Almost a century before, Edward IV had chartered this same company, granting it exceptional privileges. The policy of the Elizabethan government was merely a continuation of that of its

Many other acts of this period encourage craft organizations to exert their power to secure good workmanship. In London, for instance, only those free of the company of curriers were permitted to curry leather.[1] The wardens of the London haberdashers were given powers of search to detect illegally made wares.[2] The goldsmiths' company was authorized to see that its craftsmen placed a proper mark on all work which came from their hands.[3] Special privileges were likewise granted to specific gilds. The act of 1563 itself exempted the worsted weavers of Norwich from the operation of the apprenticeship clauses, in order that previous liberties bestowed upon that company might not be prejudiced.[4] When caps went out of fashion and cappers were becoming impoverished, an act of Parliament bade every person above the age of six years, with a few exceptions, to wear caps again.[5] In short, there is no evidence to show that craft gilds either became idle or ceased to exist in any numbers after 1563, that is, during the sixteenth century.

As another result of the act of 1563, Mr. Hibbert speaks of the amalgamation of craft gilds into one or more larger and amended corporations. But as evidence he presents the Shrewsbury records where we in turn find material to refute his theory.[6] As early as 1480, the mercers' company of that city under charter from Edward IV, afforded a spectacle of as varied and heterogeneous a combination of crafts as we find anywhere a

predecessors. This view of the case receives support also from the preamble of 8 Eliz., c. 7. See *Influence and Develop. of Eng. Gilds*, p. 91, for Mr. Hibbert's interpretation of these acts.

[1] 5 Eliz., c. 8.

[2] 8 Eliz., c. 11.

[3] 18 Eliz., c. 15.

[4] 5 Eliz., c. 4, sec. xxvii.

[5] 13 Eliz., c. 19.

[6] *Op. cit.*, p. 64.

century later. Beside the mercers themselves, the company included the ironmongers, goldsmiths, brass and iron founders, pewterers, cappers or hatters, cardmakers, haberdashers, grocers, comfet and junket makers, and finally apothecaries and physicians.[1] Nor was that by any means the first amalgamated gild in English industrial history. On the contrary, amalgamation as a feature of the gild system appeared a full century earlier, beginning as soon at least as the reign of Richard II.

At that time the movement took the form of the absorption of two or more branches of the same trade into one comprehensive company, such as London grocers, which comprised the earlier pepperers and spicers.[2] A fifteenth century example was the gild of drapers and haberdashers, which absorbed the hosiers, hatters, cappers and bracemakers.[3] In the sixteenth century, the clothworkers' company[4] combined the shearmen and fullers. In London, as in most of the boroughs, the union of such naturally related trades as the barber-surgeons served a useful purpose in putting an end to rivalry.[5]

In York we discover an interesting instance of the amalgamation of two naturally related crafts following a series of fruitless attempts to keep them separate. The marshals and smiths after years of continual strife and repeated efforts to confine their craftsmen to the duties peculiar to each trade abandoned the endeavor and obtained permission from the unwilling municipality to amalgamate.[6] Many combinations of the fifteenth and

[1] *Shrop. Arch. Soc. Trans.*, vol. viii, p. 286.

[2] Hazlitt, *Livery Cos.*, p. 189.

[3] *Ibid.*, Preface, p. 26.

[4] *Ibid.*, p. 134.

[5] *Annals of the Barber-Surgeons*, pp. 51, 69, 78.

[6] *Antiquary*, vol. ii, p. 105. The marshals, ("mareschals") were shoeing smiths.

sixteenth centuries were results perhaps of similar struggles. The cordwainers and curriers of Exeter were allowed to unite as early as 1387,[1] and the shearmen and taylors of Coventry about the same period.[2] Two centuries later in Oxford the weavers and fullers had become one company.[3]

In boroughs where craft organizations were numerous, as in Shrewsbury, Bristol, Kingston-upon-Hull and Newcastle, amalgamation sometimes took place among the less important associations. To this type belonged the Shrewsbury mercers before mentioned. In Bristol as early as 1403 we find in addition to all the separate craft gilds one consolidated company composed of the farriers, smiths, cutlers and lockyers.[4] In Kingston-upon-Hull by the end of the sixteenth century the goldsmiths, smythers, pewthers, plummers, glasiers, painters, cutlers, musicians, stationers, bookbinders and basketmakers have combined to form one gild,[5] whereas the weavers, the tailors, the joiners, the carpenters, the glovers, the coopers and the bakers are each persisting as separate organizations. Newcastle, along with its numerous special gilds, boasted in 1536 an amalgamated company of goldsmiths, plumbers, pewterers and glaziers.[6]

Was there any cause for this widespread phenomenon in craft life, other than the natural tendency to union, which had its way in spite of the rigid insistence of the times upon a division of labor?[7] This question finds a

[1] Smith, *op. cit.*, p. 331.
[2] Poole, *Coventry*, p. 31.
[3] Turner, *Records of Oxford*, p. 341.
[4] *Little Red Book*, vol. ii, p. 181.
[5] Lambert, *op. cit.*, p. 264.
[6] Walford, *Gilds*, p. 199.
[7] From the time that 37 Edward III, c. 6 prescribed that artificers should choose one mystery, and use no other, countless acts were passed by successive legislatures insisting that two or more special crafts should not be exercised by the same craftsman. Such for example were 13 Richard II, c. 12; 2 Henry VI, c. 7; 4 Henry VII, c. 3; 1 James I, c. 22.

partial answer at least in the demands made upon the companies by a popular feature of town life in the fifteenth century in the celebration of the Corpus Christi festival. Accounts of this celebration in York, Coventry, Ipswich and other places show how trades were wont to continue to furnish a part of the spectacle. At York an order of a pageant for the Corpus Christi play, in 1415, joins together among others the cutlers, bladesmiths, sheathers, sealers and bucklermakers, the tilemakers, millers, furriers, hayresters and bowlers, and the saddlers, glaziers and joiners.

Canterbury records are yet more suggestive as to the process of the amalgamation of gilds for the celebration of the festival. There for a while the Corpus Christi play had been maintained wholly at the cost of the crafts and mysteries, but for some reason they ceased to take part, "to the great hurte and decay of the seide city." As a consequence the city authorities commanded that "from hensforth every craft . . . being not corporate for their non sufficience of their crafts, be associate, incorporate and adjoyning to some other crafts moste nedynge support, yf they will not labour to be corporate within themselfe."[1]

A similar situation prevailed in Coventry. The crafts of cardmakers, saddlers, masons and painters had for "long tyme past byn as oone fellauship in beryng costys, charges and other dueties of old tyme to ther pagen . . . to the said felauship longyng," but a disagreement threatened to destroy their union. The mayor of the city intervened and restored concord, and an ordinance directed that "ev'y person of the said craftys shall pay

[1] *Report Historical MSS. Com.*, vol. ix, pp. 173-5.

all dueties customes and laufull charges that long to the pagent to the wurship of this cite."[1]

Here obviously is one occasion for the amalgamation of craft gilds. The Corpus Christi celebration was a town enterprise, toward the expense of which the crafts were expected to contribute their quota. It is also extremely probable that in some of the smaller boroughs companies combined to meet other charges devolving upon them for public purposes,[2] and that in larger communities the less important trades formed heterogeneous unions for the same end. How permanent such consolidations were, or how far combination for one object meant a corresponding union in the conduct of all craft business, we have no means of knowing. The evidence of the Ipswich records would lead us to suppose that different causes at different periods produced various amalgamations of craft gilds, all temporary in character.

In 1444[3] the Ipswich companies made up twelve different groups, which under their separate banners took part in the Corpus Christi procession. Some tendency toward the consolidation of naturally allied crafts is here visible; the goldsmiths, blacksmiths, locksmiths and bladesmiths form one combination. But in the next century the crafts have assumed the form of four very heterogeneous combinations, into which apparently all the trades then present in the city had been drawn.

[1] Sharp, *Coventry Mysteries*, p. 81.

[2] Mrs. Green, *Town Life in the Fifteenth Century*, vol. ii, p. 156, in her remarks upon the Sandwich records regards the combination of trades as a pledge to undertake certain town works, as the building or repairing of its gates.

[3] Wodderspoon, *Memorials of Ipswich*, p. 165. The mercers' company for example included the mariners, shipwrights, bookbinders, printers, fishmongers, swordsetters, cooks, fletchers, physicians, hatters, cappers, merchants.

These were known as the mercers', the drapers', the tailors' and the shoemakers' companies. This arrangement seems to have been imposed upon the crafts by town officials, since any foreigner who wished to ply a trade in Ipswich was to be assigned to one of the four companies at the discretion of the bailiffs. In 1591 a further change in the situation is suggested by an order to the clothiers, clothmakers, weavers, shearmen and dyers to form one company for the better regulation of their work and the more efficient government of apprentices and servants.[1] In all probability the older miscellaneous combinations of trades did not provide for the best interests of the cloth trade in Ipswich.

In some of the smaller towns in the sixteenth and seventeenth centuries still another phase of the amalgamation movement presents itself. In Reading,[2] for example, where the gild merchant had retained its place as a municipal institution, it comprised five distinct organizations, the Mercers and Drapers, the Cutlers and Bellfounders, the Tanners and Leathersellers, the Clothiers and Clothworkers, and the Victuallers and Innholders. These five companies included all the crafts of the town, and in the main were unions of allied trades. The use of the gild merchant gives rise to the conjecture whether in some smaller boroughs the amalgamation movement was not a return to the gild-merchant system wherein the municipality and the townsmen as a body took part in the oversight and direction of all commercial interests. This supposition finds further basis in a significant item from Devizes, in Wiltshire, where in 1614 a general

[1] Wedderspoon, *op. cit.*, pp. 174, 198.

[2] Gross, *Gild Merchant*, vol. ii, p. 208. The date of this record is uncertain, but it is thought to belong to the time of Edward VI, Mary or Elizabeth.

assembly at the Guildhall ordered that the gild of merchants anciently established should be divided into three fraternities, to be known as the Drapers, the Mercers, and the Leathersellers, and that the town authorities should apportion all the crafts among these three companies.[1]

The amalgamation movement was thus upon its first appearance a natural drawing together of trades so closely related that the most paternal of governments with all its legislation could not keep them separate. Indeed at the very time that statutes continued to insist upon the separation, both state and municipality were granting license to unite. One wonders if any effort were made to reconcile these apparently irreconcilable aspects of governmental policy, and how the contradiction affected the general respect for law, and faith in its ability to cure all human ills. The later trend toward heterogeneous combinations seems to have been the inevitable result of bearing public obligations. Later still in some of the smaller towns it betokens a return possibly to the old gild-merchant idea, and there represents, perhaps, a last attempt to keep craft organizations in existence. To attribute the whole amalgamation movement to the influence of any one statute as Mr. Hibbert does to the act of 1563, is to claim for that measure an influence which it never could have had on English industrial life.

The review thus completed of craft-gild conditions after the act of 1563 has doubtless proved that the sweeping results attributed to it are in no way confirmed by any available records. Neither the dissolution nor the amalgamation of craft gilds depends upon it. Whether the writers who lay so much stress upon the act, view it

[1] Gross, *op. cit.*, p. 55.

as a mark of hostility consciously aimed to deprive gilds of their powers, or whether they conceive the results to have followed unexpectedly as the statute was put in operation, is not always clear. There remains, however, a bit of evidence furnished by a later Elizabethan charter to an amalgamated company which must be considered in any adequate discussion of the policy of the government toward craft gilds.

In 1590 the weavers, walkers and clothiers of Worcester obtained a royal charter[1] upon a petition to the government, calling attention to the depressed condition of their trades. This charter incorporated them with the powers granted at that time to favored companies. They received the right to appoint a Council-house where a court of the master, wardens and assistants were to "treat, debate, consult and diserne of the statutes, laws, articles, and ordinances of the said misteries . . . from time to time to frame . . . such lawes, statutes, ordinances so as they be not repugnant to the laws and statutes of the Realme of England." To enforce its legislation the company was "to ordain, limit, provide, and inflict" punishments and penalties "as well by imprisonment of the body as by fine and amercements, or by any other ways, so that they be not repugnant to the laws of the Realm." The officers of the company were given oversight of all servants and apprentices of the mysteries, and the bailiffs, aldermen and other officers of the town were bidden "at the request of the said Master, Wardens and Commonalty in the execucon and exercising of the premises" to be "unto them in all things aiding and assisting." As a fitting climax to this liberality the charter ends with the clause:

[1] Green, *Hist. and Antiq. of Worcester*, vol. ii, appendix, lxxi.

These letters patent to be in all things good, firme, forceable and effectuall in law, the statute in the Parliament holden at Westminster in the 19th yeare of the reigne of our most noble grandfather, H. VII, or any other statute, ordaynances, privileges concerning the premises or any other things, causes or matter to the contrary thereof notwithstanding.

Here we have a declaration of policy in no ambiguous terms. Does it express the attitude of the Elizabethan government toward craft gilds throughout the country or an exceptional favor for this Worcester association? Although evidence fails to provide a satisfactory answer to the question, yet this guarantee of good will toward one company of no extraordinary importance surely possesses some significance, and points toward a general friendliness of sentiment on the part of the government such as we have argued throughout this investigation.

In granting to the company power to hold its court in complete disregard of the statute of Henry VII, the Elizabethan government was certainly endowing it with the widest privilege ever conferred upon a craft organization. Moreover, the entire policy pursued toward the gild system during the later sixteenth century at least, whether embodied in statutes, town records or crown charters, bears an equally favorable interpretation. The Elizabethan government was following the example of its predecessors from the days of the Normans. Not only did it issue charters directly to the crafts but it expressly commissioned boroughs to incorporate new companies.[1] All evidence of this kind unites to show

[1] A charter of Elizabeth dated 1587, permitted the mayor, bailiffs and commonalty of Winchester from time to time, to "ordain, create and establish a society, gild or fraternity, of one master and wardens of every art, mystery and occupation used or occupied," or thereafter to be "used or occupied, within the said city and the suburbs thereof." Gross, *op. cit.*, vol. ii, pp. 264, 265.

that in the eyes of the government, craft companies were not declining either in importance or value.

What then was the intention of the government in passing the statute of apprentices? As the preamble itself stated there was no idea of introducing a serious change into the industrial mechanism. The provisions had all been heard before. Their effects upon certain phases of the gild system were far less than has usually been supposed. The act was but one of a series of labor statutes passed from time to time in an endeavor to meet changing social conditions. This particular act, it is true, was more comprehensive in its nature than any that had preceded it, but it illustrated the aim of the government of the period to frame a complete system of state control. We are apt, however, to dwell overmuch upon the comprehensiveness of the system, and to omit to inquire how far the administration possessed the energy to put it into operation. The fact that the government of James I found it expedient to reiterate and expand the provisions of the act of apprentices which dealt with the assessment of wages, demonstrates that they had been by no means so forcibly or clearly enunciated before as writers have declared. Confusion still dwelt in the minds of the officials entrusted with the enforcement of the provisions that must have nullified many of the effects expected to follow the enactment. This view of the situation would itself prevent us from ascribing too great an influence to it. Moreover, in requiring a seven-years apprenticeship as preliminary to craft membership throughout the whole industrial world, the government was surely providing encouragement for gild organization and control.[1]

[1] Professor Cunningham's theory, supported by evidence from the

That the gilds continued to exercise their functions without apparent injury from the act of 1563 can safely be asserted. As far as statute and charter could preserve the powers of the craft gilds they had done so. The Worcester gild had for example received favors far more liberal than its predecessors of the fifteenth or sixteenth centuries.

Commons Journals, that the continued decay of corporate towns furnished the reason for the passage of the measure, bears out the writer's opinion that the government was much in sympathy with the gilds. Professor Cunningham indeed ventures the assertion that the act appears to have arrested the decay of corporate towns. *Modern Times*, pt. i, pp. 26, 32.

CHAPTER IV

ENGLISH ECONOMIC POLICY IN THE MIDDLE AGES

THE foregoing chapters have offered an analysis and interpretation of various legal enactments passed by the English government in its attempts to check industrial and commercial abuses as they were denounced by the public. Previous theories have credited these acts with far-reaching and fatal results upon the gild system, but these theories are for the most part refuted by the evidence herein presented and discussed. It has been shown that the gilds never actually possessed legal rights of final decision of three points with which their system was most vitally concerned, namely, the determination of prices, the rating of wages and the adoption of a required term of apprenticeship.

The gild system, as we have seen, rose and developed as an outgrowth of the peculiar conditions of mediæval life, as an organization of the forces of trade and industry which centred in England's boroughs. Organization took place there as it did in every sphere of activity in the Middle Ages. The mediæval man performed his part as a unit in some group whether he dealt with the gild, the manor, the borough, or the church. His position in one of these groups entailed upon him certain duties and obligations, but conferred, as a rule, no right to any independence of action. This was essentially the case in gild organizations. Their members had no power to initiate rules of procedure in regard to their vital interests. Neither the laws of the land nor civic authority allowed them any such prerogative.

A right understanding of the relation which existed between government, municipality and gild, and also between law and local custom, are thus necessary for a clear comprehension of the effects of any statutory enactment upon the comprehensive craft system. We meet so constantly with both custom and law in mediæval England, that it is not strange that we should sometimes fail to discriminate between them. Early industrial usage is sometimes the result of local custom supported merely by local authority, and again it is dependent upon law already promulgated and recognized as the basis for economic regulation. Both law and custom have a distinct place in the evolution of usage and a proper conception of the relation between them is essential to an estimate of the influence of any legislative act. What makes the law more effective than the custom?

As we have shown, the three chief subjects of gild concern, the questions of price, of wages and of apprenticeship, were in the beginning matters of local custom and borough ruling. Only when disturbances in the usual social arrangement took place did these subjects come up for discussion, and therefore for record. Since, however, the first disturbances were ordinarily local in character, local authority took charge and adjusted the difficulty. Occasionally the royal will made itself heard by special writ or proclamation, reminding the king's subjects that his interference was something to be feared. Not until the middle of the fourteenth century did social crises require more forcible handling than local power was able to provide. Then the confusion prevalent in the labor world demanded national action. Parliament by means of legislation undertook the restoration of order. To be sure the government exerted all its strength to keep conditions in general as they had been, but it also plainly declared that the initiative had passed from local power, and that local custom must, in case of conflict, give precedence to the new law of the realm. The land's law, not the town's law, was thereafter to be first.[1] In particular, the determination of the price of labor and of commodities became national concerns.

Long before this time certain general rules for the conduct of trade and industry had been formulated by royal edict, although not until the end of the twelfth century had the crown made itself felt as a controlling force in economic life. Then the first Assize of Measures was sent broadcast to publish the king's desire that one measure should be used in all market transactions. To facilitate compliance with the order, a quantity of standard weights and measures were distributed throughout the realm.[2] With the granting of Magna Charta royal proclamation was supplemented by statute. The charter provided not only that one measure should rule for wine and ale, but likewise one measure for corn—the London quart—and one width for dyed cloths; moreover, "with weights it was to be as with measures."[3] Somewhat later, to ensure the use of the king's standard,[4] the decree went out that the towns should affix their seals to measures within their borders. Throughout succeeding

[1] Jenks refers to the difference which existed between England and the Continent, especially Germany, in their conception of law. *Law and Politics in the Middle Ages*, p. 53.

[2] Bateson, *Mediæval England*, p. 270, from a record on a Pipe Roll of Richard II.

[3] Section 35.

[4] The statute, probably from 51 Henry III, insists that no measure shall be in any town unless it agrees with the king's measure.

reigns royal prerogative continued to exercise its privileges.[1] Following an Assize of Measures, it issued an Assize of Bread and Ale,[2] which later in the thirteenth century was also passed as an act of Parliament.

Certain offences against mediæval trade ethics were at this same time condemned by legal enactment. The sin of the forestaller was pronounced a national misdemeanor,[3] punishable as such, and soon his companions in crime, the engrosser and regrator, came in for their share of censure. Early records show the local courts engaged in enforcing these laws, and inquiring into breaches "of the assize of bread, beer, wine . . . cloths, weights, measures . . . as well as of false scales,"—interesting examples of judicial zeal.[4]

Within the boroughs, the responsibility early laid upon the authorities of enforcing these provisions, was also seriously assumed. The assizes of bread, wine and ale, gave borough officials full charge not only of weights and measures, but, as we have seen, of prices as well, and throughout the centuries borough legislation and court decisions deal frequently with violations of these market regulations. Town records teem with ordinances that bakers bake bread of proper weight or that ale be

[1] Such acts as 25 Edward I; 25 Edward III, Stat. 5, c. 10; 8 Henry VI, c. 5, relate to the subject of measures.

[2] An Assize of Bread was first proclaimed in 1202, although there is no legislative record of such an act until the statute of 51 Henry III, called the Assize of Bread and Ale.

[3] In this same statute, 51 Henry III, the forestaller was denounced as "an open oppressor of poor people and of all commonalty, and an enemy of the whole shire and country." Amercement was to be made upon one convicted of the offence, in the loss of articles purchased, according to the custom and ordinance of the town.

[4] These were articles of an inquiry to be made at a view of frankpledge in a Hundred Court, in the time of Edward I. Taken from the Mirror of Justices. Smith, *Eng. Gilds*, p. 366.

brewed according to the assize. Borough admonition and punishment are constantly required by local regrators and engrossers.[1]

Not only did national enactments confer upon borough officials control of the execution of economic laws, but municipal charters often gave them specifically the oversight of the "assize of wines, beer, ale or bread," or provided "for default of yards, balances, weights or measures that the mayor and bailiffs may have cognizance, assay, correction, and punishment in all manner of such defaults."[2] The mayor on taking his oath of office swore to maintain these assizes, and to punish forestallers and regrators.[3] That mayors did not always keep this oath may be inferred from the need of constant reiteration both in Parliament and borough of penalties for their delinquencies. In the time of Edward II, borough magistrates were so negligent in enforcing assizes concerned with articles of food, that a special act was passed forbidding any mayor to exercise a victualler's craft during his term of office.[4] Both mayors and aldermen were later amerced for breaches of this law. The

[1] In Bristol, in 1339, the Mayor's court at the Guildhall, prescribed punishment for regrators in the fishmongers' trade, and because of deceptive practices in defrauding the king of his customs in the cloth trade, appointed a special place for the housing of cloth, and special provision for its sale. *Little Red Book*, vol. ii, pp. 22, 71.

[2] Charter granted to Bristol in 1373, on its erection into a county. *Ibid.*, p. 122. Crown charters conferring such privileges are found in all boroughs.

[3] The Leicester mayor swore to "maintain the assize of bread, wine and ale, and all other maner of victualls, and the trespassers with them I shall punish as the law woll. I shall assay all maner of weights and measures . . . I shall suffer no forestaller nor regrator dwell within this town nor the fraunches of the same." Nichols, *History of Leicester*, vol. i, pt. ii, p. 39.

[4] 12 Edward II, c. 6. Statute of York.

example of municipal officials was naturally followed by craftsmen. The boroughs themselves were obliged to insist upon the constant examination of weights and measures and the designation of special places for the sale of certain commodities so as to lessen opportunities for fraudulent practices.[1]

Throughout the sixteenth century, however, borough officials were still employed to enforce the same rules, and industrial offences were still the subject of town admonitions. In 1522 the Coventry bakers were warned by the city to discontinue their transgressions.[2] In Liverpool weights and measures fell below the standard, but because of differences in the method of measuring grain, the mayor and commonalty resolved that "the old unheaped mete be had, used and allowed."[3] The municipality of Kingston-upon-Hull was invested in 1596 with special authority over transgressors of trade regulations and with power to punish them by fines or imprisonment.[4]

Thus from early times crown and Parliament supervised and regulated the industrial interests of the country. The increasing complexity of economic life called for a system of national control of ever-increasing efficiency. More minute provisions found their way into the statute-book and thence into municipal ordinances. Borough charters renewed by successive monarchs ratified existing privileges and conferred new powers. The

[1] Bristol records at the end of the fifteenth century reiterate the duties of the mayor in overseeing the bakers and the brewers, and mention the misconduct of the latter in raising the price of malt.

[2] Coventry was the scene of endless trouble because of victuallers' misdemeanors. Harris, *Life in an Old Eng. Town*, p. 106.

[3] Picton, *Liverpool*, p. 86.

[4] Hadley, *History of Kingston*, p. 453.

towns, thoroughly conscious of their importance, learned the art of protesting against government enactments when they failed to harmonize with municipal ideas. That these protests sometimes availed, is proved by clauses inserted in many measures exempting certain boroughs from the operation of various provisions. A petition for such an exemption was usually based upon a claim of "ancient custom" and commended to favor by the payment of some substantial sum.[1]

The boroughs exercised also right of appeal directly to the crown when relief was needed from any grave difficulty. Since at such times distress was usually the result of industrial complications the borough petition gave expression also to craft grievances. Thus the appeal of the York authorities to Elizabeth for relief from their customary ferm, on the ground that they were no longer able to collect it, makes clear the dependence of the borough on craft prosperity. The weavers' industry, they said, had decayed to such an extent that many weavers had fled to adjoining districts to avoid paying their quota for the city's support. As a consequence the burden upon the weavers who still remained in the city had increased until they threatened to leave also if compelled to continue paying their old ferm.[2]

The close connection between borough and gild makes difficult an attempt to determine how far the crafts exercised any powers without reliance upon municipal support. A further difficulty appears when one observes

[1] The statute of Henry IV concerning apprentices (7 Henry IV, c. 17) proved distasteful to the Londoners. When they objected to its provisions on the plea that of old every person not of villein estate could apprentice his child to any freeman, London was exempted from the operation of the act. Merewether and Stephens, *op. cit.*, p. 725.

[2] *English Historical Review*, vol. xii, p. 439.

that a great proportion of craft history is preserved only in town records. Some of the larger London companies compiled annals of considerable fullness, but they were exceptional in this as in other respects. Yet there is significance in the fact that rarely do we discover anywhere a set of craft by-laws or even a few isolated regulations which do not show signs of municipal endorsement or oversight. This statement holds as true of sixteenth century records as of any from an earlier age. When craft gilds needed confirmation of their trade regulations they asked the borough officers and the community for it. The annals of the London coopers' company record three such instances. In 1396 they applied to the municipal officers for an ordinance to restrain their craftsmen from making faulty vessels. Thirteen years later they complained to the same authorities that the offense continued and obtained rules naming the proper materials to be used thereafter. In the third year of Henry VII, the coopers again appeared before the city magistrates with the same grievance, requesting that provisions be adopted to ensure vessels of the stipulated materials.[1] The Southampton tailors, in 1474, petitioned the town officials to forbid alien tailors to ply their trade within the borough limits. They argued that the admission of foreign workmen was contrary to custom and tended to the detriment of the town's tailors and they pleaded their accustomed contributions for the town's support. It is suggestive to mark that upon the fulfilment of their request, the tailors evinced their gratitude by a substantial gift to the powers in authority.[2]

A similar device for retaining municipal favor was

[1] Firth, *Coopers Company*, pp. 5–8, 18–19.

[2] Davies, *Southampton*, p. 276.

employed in this same century by the London brewers.[1] They found the mayor, a few weeks before his retirement from office, displaying an inclination to annoy them and "assuaged his displeasure" by a handsome present. Other officers were likewise sometimes offered inducements to "be good friends to our craft." History, however, the truthful recorder of good as well as of evil, mentions one magistrate who thanked the craft masters but declined to receive their gift. In the sixteenth century the Liverpool tailors approached the municipal powers "with a douceur of fifty shillings" requesting a continuation of former exclusive privileges, and found the favor which they desired.[2] At Bristol, in the sixteenth as in the fourteenth century, the hoopers secured alterations in their by-laws from the "Mayor, Aldermen, Shrife and Common Counsaill."[3]

The clause always inserted in craft ordinances, reserving to the city officials power of interference if anything were done or attempted against the ancient customs or the city liberties, did not figure merely upon paper. Throughout the whole period, the authorities often interposed to insist upon right dealing in industrial matters. As a result of trouble in Coventry from "discevable pewter's ware," the pewterers and tanners were commanded by the Leet to sell true goods "meddled in due proportion," and masters were bidden to seal all faulty vessels and bring them before the mayor and council.[4]

Nor did the city officials fail to exercise their rights over the crafts when they objected to some craft by-law. In 1599, the bricklayers' company of Kingston-upon-

[1] Herbert, *Twelve Great Livery Companies*, vol. i, p. 57.

[2] Picton, *op. cit.*, p. 74.

[3] *Little Red Book*, vol. ii, p. 243.

[4] *English Historical Review*, vol. ix, p. 643.

Hull presented certain articles for municipal ratification, which were vetoed as "not allowed."[1] A century earlier the ordinances of the Coventry dyers[2] were declared "void, quashed and annulled." In 1524, the corporation of Coventry in a desire apparently to break down gild exclusiveness, declared that any member of any craft whatsoever might receive "what number of apprentices he would," notwithstanding any ordinance to the contrary.

The municipality could rely upon royal support in all this exercise of power. Charters and statutes had designated the borough as the agency to enforce national law. In any conflict between city officials and belligerent craft gilds, appeal to the crown invariably resulted in victory for municipal power. This was the situation in King John's day, when the Lincoln city officials confiscated the cloth of the fullers and dyers for their alleged disregard of the city's customs.[3] It was so under Henry VI, when a dispute arose between the London Merchant Taylors and the municipal authorities. A royal edict established the superior privileges of the city as conferred by its great charter. When the London goldsmiths and cutlers in the sixteenth century submitted their difficulties to Parliament the mayor was empowered by special writ to investigate the matter.[4] In 1576, a controversy between the goldsmiths' craft and their wardens was committed to the ordering of the lord mayor.[5]

Membership in a gild, either as master or apprentice, depended upon standing in the municipality. An artisan

[1] Lambert, *op. cit.*, p. 276.

[2] Harris, *Life in an Old Eng. Town*, pp. 265, 272.

[3] Seligman, *Two Chapters*, p. 61. [4] Herbert, *op. cit.*, vol. i, p. 104.

[5] *Acts of Privy Council*, 1575-77, p. 186.

must be free of the borough to be admitted into a craft. Indentures of apprenticeship to be valid must be enrolled in the borough archives.[1] Both royal charters and town ordinances regulated other matters associated with craft membership. A royal charter granted to Bristol in 1344[2] provided that no apprentice should be taken into the freedom of the city unless the master he had served could testify to his good character. At Coventry, in 1494, the apprentice upon beginning his term of service was forced to take the oath "to the franchises" of the city and to bring twelve pennies to the steward for the use of the town.[3] In 1442, the stewards of Chester were bound in the sum of forty shillings to see that no foreigner was received as a master in any occupation until he had been enfranchised.[4]

The gilds on their part accepted their responsibilities as municipal organizations. Not only did they bear their part, as we have seen, in the Corpus Christi celebration, but in all borough undertakings they assumed a fair proportion of the burden. Every set of by-laws which imposes fines for breaches of gild rules, sets apart a considerable share for the city chest. One object for which the crafts were said to exist in Shrewsbury was "the weale, rest and tranquilitie of the same towne and for good rule to be kept there."[5] At Kingston-upon-Hull

[1] A record of an indenture drawn up at Northampton in Richard II's time shows a document of great length and of many stipulations. *Archæological Journal*, vol. xxix, p. 184. The Common Council is constantly ordering apprentices to bring their indentures for enrollment upon pain of forfeit by the master. *Nottingham Records*, vol. v, p. 186. This requirement is made not only during the sixteenth century but also throughout the seventeenth. *Ibid.*, vol. v, p. 387.

[2] *Little Red Book*, vol. ii, p. 37.

[3] Harris, *op. cit.*, p. 273.

[4] Merewether and Stephens, *op. cit.*, p. 904.

[5] Hibbert, *op. cit.*, p. 36.

the compositions adopted by the mayor and burgesses and the craft gild recognized and provided for the interests of both parties.[1]

City magistrates themselves were gild members. As early as 1214 the mayor of London was chosen from the mercers' gild.[2] From 1270 until 1593 he was frequently a member of the vintners' company.[3] A special grant of Henry VIII to York committed the city government to a mayor, sheriff, aldermen and common council, the council to consist of two members from each of the principal crafts and one from each of the lesser.[4]

Temptation naturally assailed city magistrates to violate the law, especially in points connected with the trades in which they were interested. Unjust dealing of this kind proved a source of much local irritation. The citizens of Leicester, for example, in the twenty-fifth year of Elizabeth, ordained at a common hall meeting that if a victualler were elected mayor then two of the company not victuallers should be chosen in accordance with the statute of Henry VIII[5] and be sworn with the mayor to assize the price of victual; nor should the mayor alter any assize thereof without the consent of the other two persons. Eight years later, when a mayor was selected who was both a baker and a common brewer, two persons were associated with him as a statute commanded to assess the price of victuals.[6]

Craft ordinances exhibit a due respect for law and frequently quote from borough or state regulations. Thus the hoopers of Bristol provide that none of their

[1] Lambert, *op. cit.*, *passim*.

[2] Hazlitt, *Livery Companies*, Gen'l Introd., pp. 68–9.

[3] *Trans. London and Middlesex Arch. Soc.*, vol. iii, p. 448.

[4] Gross, *Gild Merchant*, vol. i, p. 111, note 3.

[5] 3 Henry VIII.

[6] Nichols, *Leicester*, vol. 1, pp. 402, 406.

trade shall "bye no Syngle withute it bere is lengthe and his thiknesse and of iiii ynche and halfe in brede without sape and other defautes and of resonable makyng for the byer and sillers accordyng to the statute made for suche vessell."[1] In Nottingham two men were accused by the gild of selling "certain tiles not well and sufficiently annealed by fire, against the form of the statute thereupon issued and provided."[2] The weavers of Kingston-upon-Hull ordered that sail cloths be of the length and weight provided by statute.[3]

Any serious neglect on the part of a craft gild to carry out government ruling was only possible with municipal approval and co-operation. This truth is illustrated by the case of the goldsmiths of Norwich.[4] In the sixteenth century they applied to the municipal authorities for ordinances, to prohibit deceptive practices in their trade and in their petition disclosed the fact that a law enacted to regulate their craft in the second year of Henry VI had never been enforced in that city.

On the whole, however, the English boroughs, despite their "gret frawnches," had "smale liberte," and stood in fear of the law of the land. The gilds, in a position still more subordinate, respected and propitiated both national and burghal law. As administrators of the land's law they kept control over market regulations for this whole period. They saw that commodities were made of proper materials and that they conformed to the standards of width, weight or measure. In case of fraud the consumer had redress from the gild tribunal as

[1] *Little Red Book*, vol. ii, p. 164. The act referred to is 2 Henry VI, c. 14.

[2] *Records*, vol. iii, p. 27. Against 17 Edward IV, c. 4.

[3] Lambert, *op. cit.*, p. 208.

[4] *Reliquary*, New Series, vol. iv, p. 208. Act of 2 Henry VI, c. 17.

well as from that of the common law.[1] But proceedings at the common law for the ordinary breaches of market regulations must have been rather unsatisfactory. Indeed, appeals on craft matters to any courts other than those of the gilds were probably slow and cumbersome. The London goldsmiths, who toward the end of the sixteenth century applied to the Privy Council to settle a controversy with their wardens, must have long been out of patience before the matter was adjusted.[2] Here perhaps is the reason for the gild's continued exercise of judicial power. It acted essentially not as a lawmaking body, but as an administrative organ interested in the maintenance of certain standards of production and the enforcement of certain rules for market transactions, and its officers were commissioned to bring transgressors to speedy justice. But it could enforce no laws without the approval and co-operation of the local powers. Above the local magnates stood the state, occasionally issuing national regulations, which also the gild took upon itself to execute.

That in turn both crown and municipality recognized the importance of the gild in the national industrial scheme has become clear during the progress of this discussion. While they admitted no large powers of gild initiative, they yet fully acknowledged their rights as organs in control of every-day market transactions. Unquestionably throughout the Middle Ages national and local policy were often lax and irregular, and the gilds were free to transgress both state and municipal laws. Yet neither government nor borough allowed

[1] A customer that complained of being defrauded by an Exeter tailor who "had never been admitted for a fre sower," had to take "hys avauntage" at the common law. Smith, *Eng. Gilds*, p. 322.

[2] *Acts of the Privy Council*, 1575-77, p. 186.

such aggressions to go altogether unrebuked. Early records show cases of amercement for violations of industrial statutes. If a merchant of the early thirteenth century sold "stretched cloth," or cloth narrower than the "due breadth," he paid his fine to the king's Exchequer.[1] If he sold wine contrary to the assize he also suffered the penalty.[2] It is true that laws were neither enacted nor enforced systematically. For that would have required a system of oversight far more complex and efficient than mediæval England could boast. Notwithstanding the government's good intention, the enforcement of a wide-reaching industrial surveillance was slow of accomplishment. Statutes were continually reenacted amid complaints of violations of the older regulations. National rules were constantly being adopted as borough ordinances, and thence were incorporated into craft by-laws to the end that the commons might not be defrauded.

Nevertheless, with the steady increase in manufacturing industries, the broadening of Continental relations and the encouragement of alien immigration, the gild system became engaged in a perpetual struggle to maintain its earlier position in the industrial world. The power of the system reached perhaps its culminating point when

[1] Madox, *History of the Exchequer*, vol. i, 566. Amercements of "some men of Esseburn for selling stretched cloth," in the fourth year of John. "Richard the Parson of Sandie for wine sold contrary to the Assise," in the third year of Henry III.

[2] In 1395 there seems to have been a general indictment at Nottingham against the tradesmen and artisans for failure to keep the assizes. Brewers are guilty because they brew against the assize; all the bakers take too much from the common people for the baking of bread; tanners sell leather not well tanned; shoemakers sell shoes too dearly; weavers and fullers ask too large a price; artisans connected with the building trades, carpenters, plasterers, stonecutters, do likewise, "against the statute of our Lord, the King." *Records*, vol. i, p. 269.

the government began to intervene, as in 1437, to check its aggressions. Yet it is a question whether with the rise of journeymen's associations the seeds of decay were not already planted within the system. As class differences were emphasized, craft organizations necessarily showed signs of the beginning of the end.

Thus the gild system declined, and a new industrial machinery, more adapted for the larger industrial life of later centuries, took its place. As an economic institution the gild system was outgrown, naturally and inevitably. What had sufficed for the thirteenth, fourteenth and early fifteenth centuries was inadequate for the sixteenth. But that the English government, thoroughly conservative in its industrial policy, was responsible, by legislative enactments, for the decline of the gild system is altogether unlikely. All the weight of available evidence shows the state encouraging the old craft companies to the last.

Conclusion

Herewith we bring to a close our study of the gild system in its relations to crown, Parliament and municipality during the period of its rise, development and decline, as also our examination of the principles of mediæval trade administration as enunciated in statutory enactments and borough ordinances. With the overthrow of the gild merchant, the earliest embodiment of the system, both town and craft organizations arose to take up its work, dividing its functions between them. Whether the gild merchant welcomed the change and gracefully yielded to the inevitable, whether the transition stage was one of passive acquiescence or of struggle, the records have not yet disclosed. We know only that municipal and craft organization were finally established, the latter amenable, commonly with no thought of resistance, to borough direction. Municipal and craft aims seemed essentially identical—so much so that in some instances craft organizations were formed at the command of burghal authorities.[1] Furthermore, the gilds actually needed municipal aid and protection to enforce their own regulations. They had no standing in the community until they were enrolled in the town records. Even when they acquired sufficient wealth and importance to obtain the added privileges conferred by a royal charter they found usually included in the document an emphatic confirmation of the rule of the municipality over craft action. In any case the borough was apt to display energetic opposition if a gild presumed too much upon a royal grant. In the rare instances where a royal charter made no special mention of municipal authority, the politic gild officials of their own accord asked for civic approbation.

The policy of the English government expressed by royal and parliamentary enactment and enforced by municipal machinery left no place for serious initiative on the part of the craft gilds.[2] Yet both government and municipality entrusted great powers to craft organizations, and they themselves usurped many privileges in their respective spheres, as this survey has amply testified. The constant reiteration of statutes concerned with

[1] The London masons were forced by the municipality to organize "because that their trade has not been regulated in due manner by the government of folk of their trade, in such form as other trades are." Riley, *Memorials*, pp. 280–281.

[2] If further confirmation of this fact were necessary, we might find it in the wording of the statute of 1437: "Masters, wardens and people of the gilds . . make . . unlawful and unreasonable ordinances as well of such things of which the cognisance, punishment and correction only pertains to the King, Lords of franchises, *etc.*"

the regulation of industry, the perpetual vigilance of the town authorities and their frequent interposition in craft practice, show that those bodies often disregarded both government and municipal ruling. Indeed, occasionally, as in Coventry, some of the crafts were driven to protest against the over-zealous interference of the borough.[1]

The act of Henry VI itself proves that craft gilds were presuming too much upon their powers, and conducting their affairs wholly in their own interests. But as we have observed, that measure brought no remedy for gild irregularities. It was but a statutory endorsement of the policy pursued up to that time by the boroughs, and made no change in craft conduct. Municipal responsibility for the gilds had been acknowledged before 1436 as fully as it was afterwards. When, in the early sixteenth century, the attention of the government was again directed to the persistent aggressions of the crafts and the inefficiency of local oversight, the highest state officials were constituted the authority, not only for the inspection and approval of craft by-laws, but also for the final trial of craft offences. The new method of endorsement, however, proved as ineffectual a restraint as the earlier custom. In all probability it was never more than a matter of form and a fee for the government officials. There is no sign that by-laws were ever rejected for their unlawful character, even though craft license at the time was at its greatest height. The two acts of Henry VIII rehearsed the act of Henry VII and called attention to the open defiance of its provision and the abuses in the internal arrangements of the gilds.

With the advent of Elizabeth all attempts to continue

[1] We should not forget that there was a great difference in the influence exerted by different crafts within the same town. The protest naturally came least successfully from the weaker associations.

by legislation the policy of her predecessors ceased. Whether the absence of such legislation was accidental or whether it represents an intentional leniency toward the gilds cannot be definitely asserted. But the comprehensiveness of the measures which were enacted to secure state supremacy in all other departments of social life, rather tends to prove that the gilds were being deliberately favored. This idea is borne out by the extraordinary grant of privilege to the Worcester craft, empowering it to disregard entirely the statute of Henry VII, the most important check on gild lawlessness then in existence. Moreover the act of 1563, far from being a cause of the decay of the system, directly encouraged the gilds by putting upon a national basis the requirement of a seven years' apprenticeship, which they, in their own way, had attempted for centuries to enforce. By exacting the long term of apprenticeship, the gilds had endeavored to exclude alien craftsmen and to gain and keep absolute control of all the processes of manufacture and exchange. The Bristol barbers, when applying for municipal authorization for their gild, asked particularly for permission to enforce by means of ordinance the requirement of a seven years' apprentice service. Considerable significance attaches, therefore, to the fact that under Elizabeth an act of Parliament for the first time includes this provision. In addition, the government continued to charter craft companies to an increasing degree perhaps throughout the Elizabethan régime, and granted besides to boroughs express permission to do the same. These are signs, at least, that the state was lending the weight of its authority to strengthen craft organizations and to preserve them in full possession of their ancient powers.

That the gilds should in turn encroach upon governmental and municipal powers was in the changing conditions of English social life quite inevitable.[1] But as far as evidence of statute-book, municipal records or craft by-laws shows, these associations of trade or industry are still to be regarded simply as "unions of artisans for purely economic purposes, always subordinate to the general laws and municipal administration."[2] This description is as true of them in the sixteenth as in the earlier centuries.[3] Mediæval England had recognized no initiatory powers of gild action and legislative enactment had taken none from them. The government was still as deeply interested as ever in keeping them in full operation.

Although in the English industrial scheme craft gilds occupied thus a subordinate place, yet in actual practice state, borough and gild presented frequently the appearance of a three-fold combination of almost equal forces working together for a common end. It is therefore not always easy to consider the gilds apart as distinct organs with their own special purposes and functions. The

[1] This is an added argument, perhaps the most conclusive of all, against the theory of the injuriousness of sixteenth century statutes. The crafts were still in the full tide of prosperity.

[2] Seligman, *Two Chapters*, p. 85. It must be remembered that all forms of trade as well as of industry were regarded as arts or mysteries, and that the merchant had also to serve his apprenticeship to his "craft."

[3] The conception of craft gilds as subordinate to state and municipality is the theme of Ochenkowski's *Englands wirthschaftliche Entwickelung*, p. 75. He particularly emphasizes the right and power of the city magistrates over those bodies, p. 78. Mrs. Green takes a similar view of the situation in "*Town Life in the Fifteenth Century*," vol. ii, p. 150, and in her review of Hibbert's *Influence and Development of English Gilds*. *English Historical Review*, vol. vii, p. 759. The conclusions reached in this investigation practically settle some of the questions Mrs. Green raises in her criticism of Mr. Hibbert's book. Miss Harris, the author of *Life in an Old English Town*, furnishes additional illustrations of the power of the municipality over craft gilds.

closeness of their connection with the government has been conspicuous throughout these pages. Three considerations which throw light upon the situation must be emphasized once more before we close.

First, we must remember that craft gilds existed chiefly in the centres of population and that their members were called upon to play a constantly-increasing part not only in industrial but also in social and political affairs. The more important craftsmen were exceedingly influential in national as well as in municipal councils and were thus able to obtain legislation in favor of their own interests. In this indirect way they exercised powers of initiative as well as of enforcement and formed a strong obstacle against legislation adverse to their peculiar system.

Secondly, we must note the all-important influence of London in the development of borough interests throughout the centuries. English boroughs were constantly petitioning for the privileges enjoyed in London. In London craft gilds were powerful enough by the fourteenth century to procure that generous supply of crown charters which marked the rise of the great livery companies. The English government soon learned to appreciate the value of such agents whose wealth and co-operation furnished new resources against financial embarrassment. Their usefulness protected them from dangerous molestation.

Thirdly, it must not be forgotten that the English industrial policy was protective in character, directed to the development of home industries which the state fostered and encouraged by every means in its power. Protection was likewise the purpose of the gild system. It formed the very foundation of gild policy. For this reason the government was interested in maintaining craft gilds in full possession of their legitimate powers.

When their deceptive practices increased so as to arouse public opinion thoroughly against them, the government was forced to intervene. It aimed not, however, at destroying its cherished industrial agents but at restraining their flagrant abuses of privilege.

Moreover, while the true cause of the end of the gild system must remain a subject for further investigation, yet certain indications in the progress of this study have perhaps suggested the nature of that cause. Even at this stage, it seems clear that when the end came, it was in no way due to government legislation or repression. The act of James I, of 1624, which destroyed monopolies, exempted "Corporacions Companies or Fellowshipps of Any Art, Trade, Occupation or Mistery," from the operation of its provisions.[1] New craft gilds were actually created after 1563. In 1571 the makers of fringe and lace in Norwich were commanded to form a gild of "parchementiers."[2] In the very year of the act against monopolies just mentioned, the cutlers' company of Sheffield received a parliamentary grant of incorporation. This charter apparently superseded one which they had obtained in 1590 from their lord, the Earl of Shrewsbury, "for the better relief and comodytie of the poorer sorte of the said fellowshippe."[3] The newly risen craft of frame-work knitters,[4] of London, was granted permission to organize by Charles II, with power to make by-laws for the government of the trade. These are but a few of the examples which might be cited.

Thus neither by unwillingness to incorporate craft companies nor by direct repressive enactment, did the

[1] 21 James I, c. 3, sec. ix.

[2] Moens, *Walloons*, p. 76.

[3] Hunter's *Hallamshire*, p. 119.

[4] Wylie, *Old and New Nottingham*, p. 293.

government ever display hostility to the gild system. Indeed the conservatism of English economic policy is shown by the failure to remove from the statute book until the nineteenth century, the mediæval restrictive legislation upon which the gild system had flourished.[1]

Such evidence as we possess bearing on the end of the English gild system is thoroughly consistent with our view of the institution as a whole. We have regarded it, primarily, not as a government creation but as an outgrowth of the municipality. It rose, developed, claimed control of the industrial life of the times and received fostering and encouragement when municipal authorities fully admitted its value. Then followed both royal and parliamentary support and the gild system grew still more in importance and power. Yet, notwithstanding national favor, its continuance in prosperity was possible only as long as local municipal conditions made it the most profitable form of organization. When borough interests could no longer be best conserved by the preservation of craft companies their death-knell was rung.[2] This stage was not reached, however, simultan-

[1] The final clauses of the act of 1563, namely those concerned with the regulation of wages and of apprenticeship, were not finally removed from the statute book until 1813 and 1814. See 53 George III, c. 40, and 54 George III, c. 96. The statutes defining the old mediæval offenses against trade, forestalling, regrating and engrossing, were not repealed until 1844. See 7 and 8 Victoria, c. 24.

[2] In 1609, extracts from the Council minutes of Nottingham show that the ordinances of the tradesmen which apparently had come up for sanction were not allowed. As the record has it, "The voyces called for the ordinances for the tradesmen to passe vnder the townes seale. The voyces are gone agaynst the allowinge of them." *Records*, vol. iv, p. 29. The Shrewsbury tanners in 1656 refused to accede to the request of the mayor to produce their composition for his perusal; with the result that the company was prosecuted by the corporation. Hibbert, *op. cit.*, p. 99. In Kingston-upon-Hull trouble arose between the masters, journeymen and apprentices, who seem to have done all in their power to

eously in all the boroughs. Gild life lingered long in the old conservative trade centres.

hamper each other, upsetting trade and disturbing the town's peace. As a consequence, the corporation refused to sign the companies' compositions, so that in the course of a few years, according to the account of the historian, the companies declined, and at length came to nothing. Hadley, *History of Kingston-upon-Hull*, p. 828.

BIBLIOGRAPHY

Archæological Journal. Publication of the Royal Archæological Institute of Great Britain and Ireland, 1845–1902. Original Documents. Indenture of Apprenticeship of the time of Richard II. Vol. xxix. 1874.

Ashley, W. J. *An Introduction to English Economic History and Theory*. 2 vols. 1888, 1893. Review of Cunningham's *Growth of English Industry* in *Political Science Quarterly*, 1891. Vol. vi. *Surveys, Historic and Economic*. London, 1900.

Bageley, Wm. "The Guilds of Gloucester." *Transactions Bristol and Gloucester Archæological Society*, 1888, vol. xiii.

Ballard, Adolphus. *The Domesday Boroughs*. Oxford, Clarendon Press, 1904.

Bateson, Mary. *Records of the Borough of Leicester*. 2 vols. London, 1899–1901. *Cambridge Records*. Cambridge, 1903. *Mediæval England*. London, 1904. (Story of the Nations.) "A London Municipal Collection of the Reign of John." *English Historical Review*, 1902. Vol. xvii.

Bickley, F. B. *The Little Red Book of Bristol*. 2 vols. Bristol, 1900.

Blomefield, Francis. *Essay Towards a Topographical History of the County of Norfolk*. 2 vols. 1805–1810.

Brand, John. *History and Antiquities of the Town and County of Newcastle-upon-Tyne*. 2 vols. London, 1789.

Brentano, Lujo. *The History and Development of Gilds*. Published with Toulmin Smith's *English Gilds*.

Busch, William. *England under the Tudors*. Translated by A. M. Todd. 1895.

Cheyney, Edward P. *An Introduction to the Industrial and Social History of England*. New York, 1901.

Clode, C. M. *Memorials of the Guild of Merchant Taylors*. London, 1875.

Crump, C. G. "London and the Gild Merchant." *English Historical Review*, 1903. Vol. xviii.

Cunningham, Wm. *Growth of English Industry and Commerce*. 2 vols. London, 1890. *Modern Times*. 3rd edition. 2 vols. Cambridge, 1903. "The Perversion of Economic History." *Economic Journal*, 1892. Vol. ii.

Davies, J. Silvester. *A History of Southampton*. Southampton, 1883.

Drinkwater, C. H. "Drapers Company Charter." *Transactions of Shropshire Arch. and Nat. Hist. Soc.* 2nd Series. Vol. viii.

England, Public Records of. Acts of the Privy Council in progress 1540–1597. Ed. J. R. Dasent, 1890–1902; Calendar of State Papers Domestic, in progress 1509; Domesday Book. 4 vols. 1783–1816; Historical MSS. Commission Publications, 1883–1904; Journals of the House of Commons, 1547–1628; Rotuli Parliamentorum. 6 vols. 1278–1503, 1767–77; Statutes of the Realm, 1101–1713, 1810–22.

Firth, James F. *Coopers Company of London*. Historical Memorandum, Charters, Documents and Extracts from the Records of the Corporation. London, 1848.

Fox, Francis F. "Some Account of the Ancient Fraternity of Merchant Taylors at Bristol with Manuscripts of Ordinances and other Documents." *Archæological Journal*. 1881. Vol. xxxviii.

Gasquet, F. A. *Eve of the Reformation*. New York, 1900.

Gilbert, J. T. *Historic and Municipal Documents of Ireland*. Rolls Series. London, 1870.

Green, Mrs. Alice. *Town Life in the Fifteenth Century*. 2 vols. 1894. Review of Hibbert's *Influence and Development of English Gilds, English Historical Review*, 1892. Vol. vii.

Green, Valentine. *History and Antiquities of the City and Suburbs of Worcester*. 2 vols. London, 1796.

Gross, Charles. *Gild Merchant*. Oxford, at the Clarendon Press, 1890

Hadley, George. *History of the Town and County of Kingston-upon-Hull*. Kingston, 1788.

Harris, Mary Dormer. *Life in an Old English Town*. (Coventry). (Social England Series.) London, 1898. "Lawrence Saunders, Citizen of Coventry." *English Historical Review*, 1894. Vol. ix.

Hazlitt, W. Carew. *The Livery Companies of the City of London*. London, 1892.

Herbert, William. *History of the Twelve Great Livery Companies of London*. London, 1837.

Hewins, W. A. S. "The Regulation of Wages by the Justice of the Peace." *Economic Journal*, 1898. Vol. viii.

Hibbert, Francis Aidan. *Influence and Development of English Gilds, as Illustrated by the History of the Craft Gilds of Shrewsbury*. (Cambridge Historical Essays.) 1891.

Hills, Gordon M. "On the Ancient Company of Stitchmen of Ludlow. Their Account Book and Money-Box." *Journal of British Arch. Association*, 1868. Vol. xxiv.

Hope, R. C. *Ordinances of the Goldsmiths of Norwich. Reliquary*, new series. Vol. iv.

Hudson, Wm. *Leet Jurisdiction in Norwich. Selden Society Publications*. Vol. v.

Hunt, W. Willmer. *Bristol* (*Historic Towns*). London, 1887.

Hunter, Joseph. *Hallomshire, in the County of York*. Edited by Rev. Alfred Gatty. London, 1819.

Hutchins, B. L. "The Regulation of Wages by Guilds and Town Authorities. *Economic Journal*, 1900. Vol. x.

Jenks, Edward. *Law and Politics in the Middle Ages*. New York, 1898.

Jupp and Pocock. *Historical Account of the Worshipful Company of Carpenters*. London, 1848.

Kemble, John M. *The Saxons in England*. 2 vols. London, 1876.

Lambert, J. Malet. *Two Thousand Years of Gild Life*, with a full Account of the Gilds and Trading Companies of Kingston-upon-Hull. Hull, 1891.

Latimer, John. *Annals of Bristol of the Seventeenth Century*. Bristol, 1900.

Leach, Arthur F. *Beverley Town Documents*, (*Selden Society Publications*). London, 1900.

Leighton, W. A. "The Gilds of Shrewsbury in Shropshire." *Arch. and Nat. Hist. Soc. Trans.* Vol. viii.

Madox, Thomas. *The History and Antiquities of the Exchequer*. 2 vols. London, 1759.

Maitland, Frederic Wm. *Domesday Book and Beyond*. Cambridge, 1897.

McArthur, Ellen A. "'The Boke Longyng to a Justice of the Peace' and The Assessment of Wages." *English Historical Review*, 1894. Vol. ix. "A Fifteenth Century Assessment of Wages." "Prices at Woodstock in 1604." *English Historical Review*, 1898. Vol. xiii. "Regulation of Wages in the Sixteenth Century." *English Historical Review*, 1900. Vol. xv.

Merewether and Stephens. *History of the Boroughs and Municipal Corporations of the United Kingdom*. 3 vols. London, 1835.

Milbourn, Thomas. "Biographical Notices of Some Eminent Members of the Vintners Company." *Transactions of the London and Middlesex Archæological Society*. Vol. iii. 1871.

Moens, William J. C. *The Walloons and their Church at Norwich. Publications of the Huguenot Society of London*. Vol. i. 1887-8.

Nicholl, John. *Some Account of the Worshipful Company of Ironmongers of London*. London, 1851.

Nichols, John. *The History and Antiquities of the County of Leicester*. 4 vols. Leicester, 1795-1815.

Nichols, J. G. "The Muniments of the Vintners Company." *Transactions of the London and Middlesex Archæological Society*, 1871. Vol. iii.

Norton, George. *Commentaries on the History, Constitution and Chartered Franchises of London*. London, 1869.

Ochenkowski, W. von. *Englands wirthschaftliche Entwickelung im Ausgange des Mittelalters*. Jena, 1879.

Overall, Wm. H. "Some Account of the Ward of Vintry and the Vintners Company." *Transactions of the London and Middlesex Archæological Society*, 1871. Vol. iii.

Picton, James A. *Selections from the Municipal Archives and Records of Liverpool from the 13th to the 17th Centuries*. Liverpool, 1883.

Poole, Benjamin. *Coventry. Its History and Antiquities*. London, 1870.

Riley, H. T. *Memorials of London and London Life in the XIII, XIV and XV Centuries*. London, 1868. *Munimenta Gildhallae Londoniensis*. Rolls Series. 4 vols. *Liber Albus*, 1859. *Liber Custumarum*. 2 vols. 1860.

Seligman, Edwin R. A. *Two Chapters on the Mediæval Gilds of England*. *Publications of the American Economic Association*. 1887.

Sellers, Maud. "The City of York in the Sixteenth Century." *English Historical Review*. 1894. Vol. ix. "York in the Sixteenth and Seventeenth Centuries." *English Historical Review*. 1897. Vol. xii.

Sharp, Thomas. *A Dissertation on the Pageants or Dramatic Mysteries Anciently Performed at Coventry*. Coventry, 1825.

Smith, J. Toulmin. *English Gilds*. Original Ordinances of more than 100 early English Gilds. *Early English Text Society Publications*. London, 1870.

Smith, Lucy T. "Ordinances of the Companies of Marshals and Smiths at York." *Antiquary*. Vol. ii. "The Bakers of York and Their Ancient Ordinary." *Archæological Review*. 1888. Vol. i.

Stevenson, W. H. *Records of Nottingham*. 5 vols. Nottingham, 1882-1900.

Stubbs, William. *The Constitutional History of England in its Origin and Development*. 3 vols. Clarendon Press. Oxford, 1874. *Select Charters and Other Illustrations of English Constitutional History*. 1895.

Thompson, Pishey. *History and Antiquities of Boston*. Boston, 1856.

Transactions of the Bristol and Gloucester Archæological Society. Vol. viii. 1884. *The Gild of Weavers of Cirencester*.

Turner, Wm. H. *Selections from the Records of the City of Oxford*. 1501-1583. Oxford and London, 1880.

Walford, Cornelius. *Gilds.* London, 1888.

Western Antiquary, or Devon and Cornwall Note-Book. Edited by W. H. K. Wright. Plymouth, 1882-1893. 12 vols. *Gilds of Exeter.* Vol. iv.

Wiltshire Notes and Queries. An Illustrated Quarterly Antiquarian and Genealogical Magazine. 3 vols. Devizes. *Guild of Tailors of Salisbury.* Vol. i.

Wodderspoon, John. *Memorials of Ipswich.* Ipswich, 1850.

Wylie, Wm. H. *Old and New Nottingham.* London, 1853.

Young, Sidney. *Annals of the Barber-Surgeons of London.* London, 1890.

Bei Fragen zur Produktsicherheit wenden Sie sich bitte an:
If you have any questions regarding product safety,
please contact:

Walter de Gruyter GmbH
Genthiner Straße 13
10785 Berlin
productsafety@degruyterbrill.com